Impassable Canyon

Journey Down the Middle Fork of the Salmon

Photography Matt Leidecker

Essays
Cort Conley
Peter Gibbs
Erik Leidecker
Matt Leidecker
Greg Moore
William Studebaker

Poetry
David Wagoner

Foreword
Clarence Stilwill

Sun Valley Press
a division of
Valley Publishing LLC
Hailey, Idaho

SUN VALLEY PRESS
a division of
Valley Publishing LLC
12 East Bullion Street
Suite B
Hailey, Idaho 83333
208.788.0770
www.sunvalleymag.com

Editor
Laurie Sammis

Art Director/Book Design
Randi Pallan

Photo Editor
Lauren MacLaughlin

ISBN 0-9724911-0-4
Printed and bound in South Korea

Library of Congress Control Number: 2002114158
Leidecker, Matt Impassable Canyon: Journey Down the MIddle Fork of the Salmon

1. Photography 2. Leidecker, Matt 3. Middle Fork 4. Salmon River

First Printing: November 2002

Special thanks to Bob Sevy
and his Middle Fork crews for
all they have taught me
about rivers.

M.L.

Contents

Foreword

by Clarence Stilwill

WHEN MATT FIRST CALLED ME and set forth the editorial guidelines for this book, it was spring and the rivers of the West were beginning to flow. In fact, Matt hadn't much time to talk because he was on his way to do a Jarbidge/Bruneau trip and, after that, another Owyhee Canyon run much like the one from which he had just returned. From there he would be going on to the Middle Fork to start the summer season.

Ah, rivers! When we hung up I was struck with longing, almost a physical pang . . . Could I call him back and ask to hitch on? My old Miwok was rolled up in the corner of the barn, its rusty steel frame hanging from a nail. The 12-foot ash oars were stored across the rafters, gathering dust. I consulted my maps and my memories.

After thirty years, could I still cut it? Could I take on the left wall at Widowmaker, or would I stare at it too long, over thinking until my guts were gone and I'd have to line the boat around? Could I make the pull at Whistling Bird, afterward to sit sweating, shaken, and triumphant in the quiet pool below? The same pool where, years ago, I had found Byron Cadey's corncob pipe, a six-pack of beer, and a package of bacon, all swirling quietly together in a back eddy. (This peaceful little gathering belied the violent tale of a bad turnover on the trip ahead of us, one with guides, guests, and gear scattered from hell to breakfast.)

As I harvested the offering I sent my thoughts downriver, wishing them all well—a camp with good firewood and dry sleeping bags. Then, like any guide worth his salt, I tamped Byron's pipe with my own tobacco, fried his bacon, and drank his beer, all the while heaping blessings on the river gods, both his and mine.

Later, when Byron and I pulled an oar together as guides and friends, we would often laugh at my little appropriation. And then, after one last trip together, his laughter was stopped forever by the Salmon River in spring flood. He was lost, never to be discovered. Yet I know that his bones softened to water, and that he flowed with the rivers he loved to the sea—leaving me, in the intervening years, to search the quiet back eddies for a corncob pipe.

By the time I finished reviewing Matt's editorial guidelines, I was once again land bound, knowing I could not unfetter from my present life to go chasing a downriver dream that seems always one bend ahead. Yet neither could I halt the torrent of memories: Staring at the dying embers of a thousand campfires in the deep and distant canyons of the West had left me with a stockpile of river moments that had been untouched for a long while. Memories of people, of triumphs, and fears. Memories infused with moments of glory, grace, gladness, and even a few regrets, all set in places of indescribable beauty.

Opposite:
A lone kayaker is dwarfed by the granite walls of Impassable Canyon.

Although it was suggested that this foreword might attempt to capture the "essence of a river," my thoughts instinctively pointed more toward the "essence of those who float rivers," whether for joy or profit or a combination. The writers that follow, among them many with whom I have happily shared river experiences, are better equipped to deliver the "essence of rivers." Through stories and essays, in combination with Matt's photos, they present their accumulated knowledge and firsthand impressions of a life and lifestyle that, once lived, never leaves those who have participated in it. Cort Conley and Pete Gibbs now have careers unrelated to floating, but their histories and, I suspect, their futures will always be entwined with the lore of rivers.

Most of us old river runners have moved on to other things, but for some, life and rivers are inseparable. To use a cliché, it's who we are. The Helfrich brothers from Oregon learned the secrets of rivers at their father's knee. Jerry (Snake) Hughes graduated from a wild young Colorado River guide to a respected outfitter. Bob Sevy, with probably the greatest working knowledge of the Middle Fork of the thousands who have run it, started guiding, with more guts than good sense, as a teenager with the Boy Scouts, using equipment they wouldn't let you unload from the trailer these days. These men are still at it, sharing over a hundred years of accumulated river-running experience among them.

There is a point in boating, and it is a magical point, when one becomes intimate with a certain river. It extends beyond the position of mere familiarity with the rapids, or competence and proficiency at choosing campsites, good lunch spots, or side canyon trips. When truly intimate with a river, you can tell at one glance, barring freak circumstance, what is happening on it from where you stand to where it ends. The writers and river runners mentioned above have that sort of relationship with many rivers—the accumulations of a lifetime of floating. I can admit to that intimacy with a few rivers in the west: the Snake River, certain sections of the Owyhee, and also, the Middle Fork of the Salmon. When this happens, the river becomes a permanent part of your life. You may leave a river that you love, but it never leaves you.

I confess though, and I suspect that many other experienced river runners would, too, that I know nothing about numbers and their relationship to water and river canyon conditions. If the gauge at the Middle Fork Lodge reads X feet, or the predicted cfs volume on June 15 is X, to me, it's meaningless.

That's where the magic of intimacy comes in. After years of running the Middle Fork, as we unloaded the boats and gear I could study one rock mid-river at the base of Dagger Falls and read from it the next hundred miles of river. A brief observation of the water flow around that single rock could map out our next five to seven days, revealing how many river hours the party would have to spend to keep on schedule, what campsites, high or low, would be available, and what shape they would be in. It could even tell us where and how long we could dawdle for lunch or a swim.

That rock was a crystal ball in which the immediate future could be read. If water poured over the top of it, there was no way we could make the left sneak at

Velvet: We were resigned to running the falls dead center. It could answer the question of left, right, or center at Sulphur Creek, and tell us where to place the guests and with which guide (having quietly assessed their ability on the bus ride in, or at dinner in Stanley the night before). With a paddleboat crew, the rock told me how soon I would have to scare the bejesus out of them to point out the serious, life-and-death side of the adventure ahead. The flow around the rock predicted whether we were likely to play hell keeping the sweep boat off the wall at Pistol Creek rapid or wipe an oar off a raft at the bottom of Powerhouse. Intimacy with the river allowed my mind to flow five days and 80 miles downriver to see an edgy dodge through the rock field at Haystack, a backbreaking pull on Sevy's Nose, and the inescapable holes in Redside. It might begin the worry that the standing waves in Rubber were already timing themselves to flip a boat, an event I had seen a dozen times.

As a predictor, the rock could also bring good tidings—the lovely, quiet, and subtle things that always mix with the excitement of running whitewater. It would tell us if the riverside hot springs had emerged from the cold water, offering solace to tired rowing muscles; or if little shooting stars would be nodding on the bank in shady corners, or overhanging gardens dripping melodically into quiet pools—secrets revealed only to the observant and worthy.

There were some events the rock could not predict, but an experienced guide knew they could show up anywhere on the trip. Events like hurricane-force winds driving boats into the bank; lightning, thunder, and horizontal rain in brief, violent bursts out of a seemingly bright blue sky—or, at night, those same forces dropping huge trees throughout camp, tapping into a guide's worst fear, that someone could die in the act of being introduced to this beautiful wilderness.

Nor could the rock predict those hushed moments of slanted evening light when the campfire smoke hangs midlevel in the ponderosa pines at Hospital Bar. Or, seen from the hot springs above camp, the river pooling almost at a standstill, peacefully reflecting the first evening stars before slipping quietly away on its passage to the sea. Or best of all, a downriver moment when your boat finds itself alone on the river, either ahead of or behind the others in your party: All conversation stops, and as you rest on your oars, each person in the raft adrift with their own thoughts, you know that they get it, and that you are wordlessly sharing the reasons you love and live this life. Not just the challenge of matching arm and oar against the inevitability of water flowing downhill, but the matching of your spirit to this moment.

So, there you have it—a foreword of sorts. I can leave the poetics of the "essence of rivers" in the capable hands of those that follow, and in Matt's wonderful photography. "The essence of river runners" I can distill to the flow of water around a single rock, and to the life lessons learned from floating: staying present with each day, experiencing excitement and quietude in equal measure; knowing something of the future, yet reveling in mysteries unrevealed. And fearing not, for the only thing certain in life is that waiting somewhere downriver for all of us . . . is a quiet back eddy and a corncob pipe.

Following Spread:
A spectacular sunset fills the canyon with radiant purple light near Survey Camp at mile 75.

Left to Right (from top):
Indian Paintbrush.
Elephant Head and Camas.
Yellow Salsafie.
Lupine.

Bruce Meadows blooms a different color every week
during spring and early summer.

Introduction

by Matt Leidecker

IN THE SUMMER OF 1991, I began working with a whitewater rafting company on the Middle Fork of the Salmon River. My father, who worked for Bob Sevy and Sevy Guide Service in the 1970s, had taken the family on a handful of rafting trips in central Idaho, but I had never floated the Middle Fork. Through a contact with my high school biology teacher, John Cole, Bob Sevy hired me to work as the "swamper," or camp helper, with his Middle Fork crew that first summer. Twelve years later, I still find myself on the river.

The Middle Fork has become a second home to me. I have floated the length of its whitewater canyons more than a hundred times, running Marsh Creek in the spring and Dagger in the fall. I have felt the exhilaration of high water in June and the frustration of low water in August. I have flipped, pulled, wedged, spun, floated, stuck, and grunted my way downstream. While in college, I wrote my geology thesis on the Middle Fork terraces, mapping their height above the river and hypothesizing linkages to glacial history. I spent eight days in an inflatable kayak on the Middle Fork in October of 2000 after the August fires had shut the canyon down. I have hiked or run many stretches of its trails, and have even thrashed my way from the Bighorn Crags down Ship Island Creek to the river.

About five years ago, I began seeing the canyon through an entirely different perspective—a camera lens. I wanted to capture the essence of the Middle Fork and share the experience of being on the river day in and day out. My search for images took me deeper into the nooks and crannies of the river corridor. As I used my knowledge of the landscape to compose and capture photographs of light moving through the canyon, I saw more than ever before. The desire to share the fruits of those explorations of the Middle Fork's many moods and colors continued to grow, and has finally culminated in the publishing of this book.

Just as a river system is more vast and expansive than its main stem, the experience of the Middle Fork encompasses far more than what can be shown through a camera lens. The images in this book represent only one perspective of the river. Throughout these pages, sprinkled among my photographs, you will find essays and stories, drawings and quotes that complement the pictures and fill in the gaps left by film.

The talented group of writers who contributed to this book all have some connection to the Middle Fork. Like me, they have developed a strong and timeless bond with the river and her canyons, carrying her deeper meaning into their daily lives. In their writings and sketches, musings and quotes, they reflect on ideas and themes central to the vision of this book.

First and foremost is the concept of wilderness. The Middle Fork and the Frank Church River of No Return Wilderness comprise the largest chunk of federally-designated "wilderness" in the lower 48 states. Central Idaho supports one of the last complete and relatively undisturbed natural ecosystems in our country. What does this mean to modern-day humans, and what has it meant to historical inhabitants of the river system?

The second theme threading through this book is the concept of a river system in its entirety. While the photographs are largely confined to the river corridor, the essays attempt to broaden the scope and paint a larger picture. The Middle Fork is far more than just the stretch of water from Boundary Creek to Cache Bar: There are hundreds of miles of tributaries, some of which can be boated for their own merits. The Middle Fork River system encompasses both minute and catastrophic changes in geography and geology—trails, towering cliffs and etched canyons, enlivened by the calls and prints of bighorn sheep, mountain goats, coyotes, bear, mountain lions, foxes, eagles, wolves, falcons, hawks, salmon, rainbow trout, and many other creatures native to Idaho's wilderness.

Finally, we have tried to capture the essence of the experience of floating down a river. Floating the Middle Fork is a profoundly different experience from walking or riding a horse along its cliffs or banks. Boating is a fantastic way to weave through country and see landscapes that might otherwise be difficult or impossible to reach. Packing up and moving with the currents each day, then camping along the banks at night, watching the stars track across the sky and falling asleep to the gurgle or roar of moving water, provides a more intimate experience of the river's ebbs and flows.

In discussions and interviews related to this book, I spoke with a man named Bill Wexelblatt, from Piedmont, California. He said this about the Middle Fork:

> "You wake up in the morning and you know exactly what your day is going to be like. At the same time, you also know that something will happen that has probably never happened on the river before."

To me, this quote expresses the true essence of the Middle Fork. While on the river, my eyes are open; I notice all of the sights and sounds, and learn something new with each adventure. On the Middle Fork, every trip is an experience.

Upper Canyon

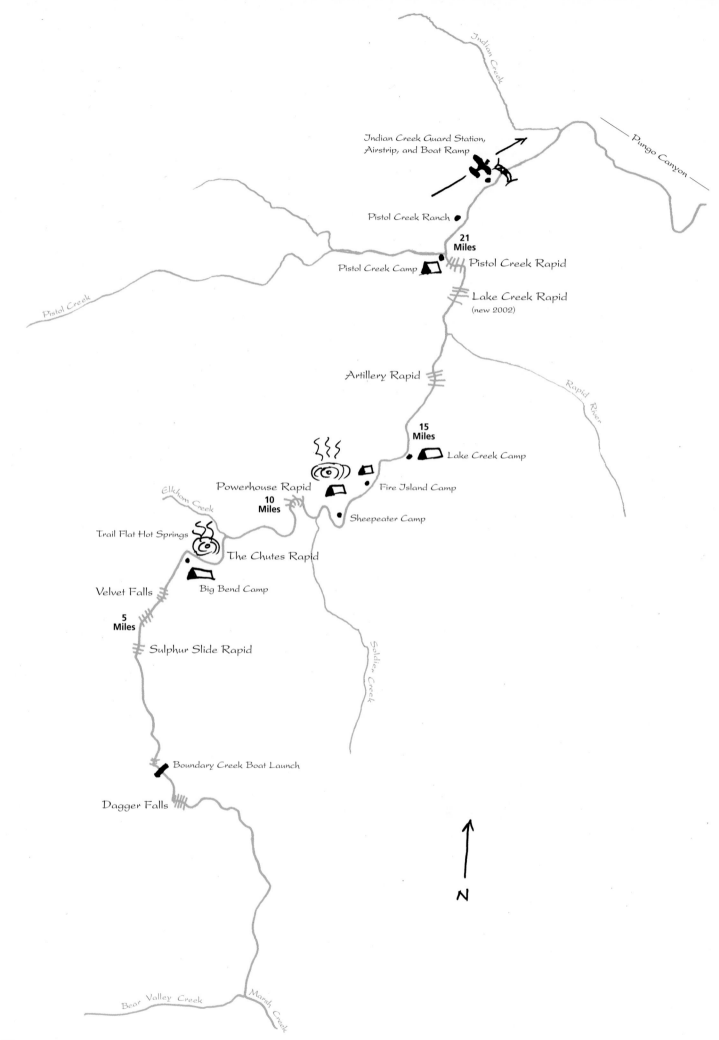

Indian Creek Guard Station,
Airstrip, and Boat Ramp

Pungo Canyon

Indian Creek

Pistol Creek Ranch

21
Miles

Pistol Creek Camp

Pistol Creek Rapid

Lake Creek Rapid
(new 2002)

Pistol Creek

Artillery Rapid

Rapid River

15
Miles

Lake Creek Camp

Powerhouse Rapid

Fire Island Camp

Elkhorn Creek

10
Miles

Sheepeater Camp

Trail Flat Hot Springs

The Chutes Rapid

Velvet Falls

Big Bend Camp

Soldier Creek

5
Miles

Sulphur Slide Rapid

Boundary Creek Boat Launch

Dagger Falls

N

Bear Valley Creek

Marsh Creek

Upper Canyon

by William Studebaker

ON COLD, EARLY-SPRING mornings, the road to the Upper Middle Fork's official put in is blocked by snow, so boaters launch on Marsh Creek, some 25 minutes west of Stanley just off Highway 20. It's a shallow start, but Marsh picks up quickly, and Bear Valley Creek dumps in before long, forming the fledgling Middle Fork of the Salmon River. There are roughly ten more downstream miles before Dagger Falls and the Forest Service put in at Boundary Creek.

At Boundary Creek there are both boat launch and trailhead, but you must leave your engines, wheels, and brakes behind, and go by oar, paddle, hoof, or foot. Any apprehension will soon be whisked away by the alluring prospect of the rugged river and the largest wilderness in the lower 48 states: the Frank Church River of No Return Wilderness Area.

During late-spring snowmelt and throughout the summer, the Forest Service dirt road is open. You can just drive up, put in, and, within two strokes from the boat ramp, enter the wilderness.

Inside, mountains like Big Soldier, 8,980 feet high, claim their place above the clouds. The river continues to drop, producing some of the finest outback whitewater in the country. The water is forced through articulate bedrock, landslides, and creek-slender alluvial deposits formed as recently as yesterday. What to call the Upper's pathway is hard to say. It's a paradoxical place—high forest and steep river, never as wide as a valley, never as vertical as a canyon, but the sheared banks of an S-turn seem to crisscross behind you. The mountains rise and lean nearly straight up, right from the river's center, and there are just enough flats where cobbles have been piled to allow room for a few camps.

The Middle Fork trail follows the river—when it can. Sometimes it goes up, over the top of a cliff and through the woods. It has a way of wandering, moving about on its own, in and out of lush raspberry bushes, across rivulets, near fern fronds, and past abandoned mining claims. You might see a tranquil mountain boa, a true constrictor, resting there on its buttery belly with its milk chocolate back glistening in the sun of the trail. (Should you, against good advice, choose to pick it up, study the head for as long as it takes to tell it from the tail.)

The Upper is an easy journey—if you like steep, if cool and green mean anything to you. And almost anywhere you might want to stop, you can put your feet into cold, rushing water—or, on some nights, hot.

Rapids like Powerhouse offer a good punch, combining a twisting route and high-speed descent. The pace isn't too fast for history, though: Still lining the river are the old powerhouse, cabin, and sundry buildings built by prospectors in search of ore. Placer tailings next to Sheepeater Camp and near the mouth of Greyhound Creek represent more signs of the old prospectors' get-rich-quick dreams.

Somewhere between Pistol Creek and Marble Creek, maybe at Indian Creek, which is more than 25 miles from the end of the road, the Upper gives way, surrendering the forests of a high alpine paradise to the wandering horizons of the Middle Canyon.

Sheepeater Creek on a summer afternoon.

Preceding Spread:
Smoke from a nearby forest fire stretches into fingers of haze and isolates the pine-covered ridgelines downstream from Fire Island Camp.

A patch of late-spring alpine shooting star hugs an eddy near the Boundary Creek launch ramp.

Preceding Spread:
A group of excited youngsters experiences Middle Fork whitewater.

Stitching the River to its Shore

by Cort Conley

ONLY HALF A DOZEN SOULS—caretakers, really—now winter on the Middle Fork of the Salmon River. Before its touristification, however, with rafts thick as ticks, the river did have a resident population significantly larger than at present. For these inhabitants, overwhelmingly male, the Middle Fork was the canyon of their homes, the canyon of their chores, the canyon of their stories.

Who were they? Men accustomed to doing things for themselves. Why did they choose the Middle Fork? The pull of the current and, likely, the calculus of chance. What were they looking for? A determined privacy at a private anchorage. What did they do? Mined, trapped, packed. Did they consider it a special place? In the same sense that one river differs from all others. Why did they leave? Probably because the river washed its hands of them.

There can be no doubt that these men, who preferred to drink upstream from the herd, were eccentric characters: Cougar Dave, Dutch John, Whitie Cox, Settrigger Purcell, Beargrease Falconbury. In an essay, John Stuart Mill argued that "eccentricity has always abounded when and where strength of character abounded." Although we are now removed by more than half a century from their streamside tidemark, it still may be possible to puzzle out their shared characteristics—traits less noticed or remarked upon then than now.

From the launch ramp at Boundary Creek, going north with the river's slant, within two miles a boater can moor at Sulphur Creek on river left. The stream runs through the old Fuller homestead. Jim Fuller was born in a wagon train as his mother crossed Nebraska. Years later, as a young man trailing cattle in 1904, he turned down into the Middle Fork canyon and discovered the site he wanted to homestead, and did. He and his wife lived there spring and summer with five children, trailing cows for the Sulphur Creek Cattle Association.

Ten miles farther downstream, Sam Sibbetts built a waterwheel in 1913 as a power source for a one-stamp mill. He chipped away, like a river current, at the ore on the nearby mountainside and packed it down from his White Goat claim, but the mill never thumped because the river flow had dropped below the rim of the wheel by the time it was completed.

At Soldier Creek, a mile downriver, Joe Fox and Roscoe Dodge mined in the 1930s. In six weeks they shoveled out an impressive diversion ditch to sluice water to their placer claim. When ice capped the mining season, Dodge trapped mink and marten. He and Fox finally gave up, referring to the stint as a "starve-out affair" ever afterwards.

At the eddy upstream from Pistol Creek Rapid, ten miles north, Ed Harrington, Robert Teachout, and Ed Pickhardt filed a mining claim in 1938. They cut lodgepole on the site and augered a quarter-mile of sleeved, wooden pipe in ten-foot lengths. Then they contoured a ditch from Lake Creek to their pipeline, powering a small apparatus that bucketed sand and gravel into their sluice box. A meager amount of gold was recovered before Harrington, accused of bogus mining-stock sales, fled to South America. His pards soon scattered as well.

Just across the river, Sam Hoppins, half Scot, half Cherokee, settled in 1892. He ran a pack train of buckskin mules for miners and ranchers, sold out in 1914, and died from a gunshot wound inflicted by a myopic hunter who said he mistook him for a black bear.

Pungo Creek tumbles into the Middle Fork twenty-seven miles below Boundary Creek. An old-time trapper, John Minshew, native of North Carolina, took up a quartz claim at the mouth of the creek. In 1929 he had lost his job as a boiler mechanic for the Union Pacific Railroad. Retreating to the Middle Fork, he built two cabins and cultivated a large garden. In the 1940s, when his son was killed in an airplane crash on the river, Minshew abandoned the claim. Shortly thereafter, the "quartz" proved to be acid-grade fluorspar, a rich deposit, but too distant from market.

Five miles farther downriver and two miles up Marble Creek, Billy Mitchell settled at the turn of the last century. Once a miner, he switched to cattle ranching. For over thirty years he lived in a log house on the flat next to the creek, proving up on his homestead in 1923. In 1950 he sold his acreage to the Idaho Department of Fish and Game, moved to Riggins Hot Springs, and died within a year.

On the opposite side of the river, a mile from Marble Creek, Englishman Jim Voller, the "buckskin boy," settled at the mouth of Thomas Creek in 1890. He took title to his eighty-acre homestead at age fifty-nine. Higher up the creek, he dug a ditch along the knee of the hill almost half a mile in order to irrigate his sixty acres of clover. He dressed logs, hewed out a small cabin and a barn, and strung a tramway across the river. Voller kept horses, cows, and chickens, laboring without pause or praise sunlight to starlight. When his health began to unravel, he sold out to cattle ranchers, dying soon afterwards in Lewiston, Idaho.

On the flat across from Voller's place, Charley Meyers, too, owned a trim cabin and barn. Born in 1859, Meyers was a mountain man with a prophet's white beard and shoulder-length hair. His awkward gait was the consequence of a leg injury inflicted when his horse rolled over on him on a switchback of the Thunder Mountain trail. He packed in summer, trapped in winter, sipped whiskey year round, and lived into his late seventies.

Three meandering miles more, across on the east shore at Little Creek, a seedling stream, stands Hash Flat, occupied from 1900 to 1906. Missouri-born Jim Hash grew up on his father's ranch near Idaho Falls. He lived on the flat with his wife Belle, from Tennessee. Together they raised tons of potatoes and sacked them onto two-dozen burros loose herded to the miners working on Thunder Mountain. When the boom played out, the Hashes moved on to Battle Mountain, a newer mining camp in northern Nevada.

Over the next ten miles, as the river jinks left and right, right and left, again and again, there are numerous abandoned or reverted homesteads. Kenney Cameron's: Scottish immigrant—miner, packer, stockman—who left for a mule ranch in Emmett, Idaho. Charlie Rochlan's: on Little Loon Creek six miles from the river; a fur farmer raising fox and mink. So lonely he trained a pine marten to eat with him at the dinner table. Dutch John Helmke's: a German immigrant cultivating twenty-five acres at Cougar Creek from 1908-1921, selling his hay and produce at the Loon Creek mines, died at eighty-nine and was buried on his place. Rupert Falconbury's: came from Indiana in 1907, bought squatter's rights to a cabin and seventy-three acres ten miles up Loon Creek. He trapped marten (sans table manners) and fox, bobcats, and coyotes.

At the mouth of Loon Creek (mile 50), Bob Ramey patented a homestead in 1916, when he was thirty-four. He kept more than a hundred head of horses and harvested sixty tons of hay every summer.

Six miles farther down, Grouse Creek spills with a watery rustle into the river. In 1917 Willis Jones stumbled across this benign incline in a predominantly perpendicular area, and at age forty occupied the empty cabin perched at the

photo courtesy Cort Conley

photo courtesy Cort Conley

suffering from consumption, Jones farmed fifteen acres in hay, wheat, and corn. When he sold out in 1930, he drifted south to Arizona to spend the lag-end of his life.

Five miles more on river right, Clarence Kaufman, a failed miner, lived in a shallow cave fronted with a wooden door. His skill as a single-jacker carved out his single room. Kaufman left to visit a doctor and never returned.

Mile 65, river left: In 1917, on the terrace that tilts toward the river immediately upstream from Sheep Creek, lived Minnesota-born Julius Reberg. He kept horses and cattle, raised hay, placer mined for gold in the creek. In May 1917, he failed to register for the draft under the first Selective Service Act. A suspicious and covetous interloper murdered him with a shot from his Winchester carbine.

Three miles north at Brush Creek, George and "Ma" Crandall, working daybreak to backbreak, fenced a ranch at the head of Impassable Canyon and ran cattle. It was like submarine duty: In sixteen years they never left the place, but it, too, proved to be a "starve-out proposition." They retired to Arizona. George, twenty years younger than "Ma," was murdered for the money he inherited from her.

Vociferous Big Creek links up with the Middle Fork twenty miles upstream from where that river feeds the Main Salmon. Dave Lewis, born in New Orleans in 1844, lived four miles up the creek at Soldier Bar. As early as 1909, he was there alone in a four-square log cabin with a sod roof. He packed spring and fall for miners, summer fire season for the Forest Service. Lewis hunted mountain lions for the state bounty, killing a dozen or more every winter. In 1928, he secured the homestead certificate for his place, then eight years later died of pneumonia at ninety-two.

Ten miles deeper into the canyon, Nugget Creek chains down to the river. From the early 1900s until 1942, Earl Parrott—the hermit of Impassable Canyon—roosted in a hanging valley well above the river. Out of sight of the twentieth century, this inland castaway tanned hides, tended a trophy garden, and traveled nimbly down log ladders to pan gold while squatting on his haunches at the river's edge. In summer, his days blended uneventfully under a shell of blue; in winter, he hibernated under a roof of white. By choice he was as independent and self-sufficient as it is possible to be in a sealed world, his only visitors accidental and unwelcome. In 1945, age seventy-five, he died of a coronary occlusion at a hospital in Salmon, Idaho.

Given these slender particulars, what then can be said about these settlers as a group? The campfire question, endlessly recurrent, is whether they would have stood out in an urban setting. Do they, in other words, stand out because of who they were or because of where they were? Without the Middle Fork, would their songs have ended on a different note? Conclusions are somewhat vaporous because the less one knows, the more room there is to guess, and there is a lot of guesswork: The details have not weathered well.

The Middle Fork attracted three principal types: born survivors, pertinacious opportunists, and last-call homesteaders. Possessed of a resourceful courage, the survivors were ready, willing, and able all at the same time, dependent only on fish and game and firewood. They lived in cabins unpainted and unplumbed, cabins now long gone to fire or snow. In a time when no planes flew over, no boats floated past, when nothing moved faster than a horse, they found a way to scratch out a living—packing, trapping, mining—with all the endurance of a mountain mule.

The opportunists discovered ungrazed or fertile ground, relic areas within a yonder region already largely given over to sheep and cattle and crops. Setting their jaw against a more civilized society, they had to work with untiring ferocity; trail or pack farther than others; overcome blank prospects with roseate hopes. Even the federal land office recorder admitted in writing in 1920, "The winter season in this vicinity [upper Middle Fork] is so severe that nothing can be accomplished by remaining on the land, nor can any work of improvement or cultivation be done." In the end, the opportunists often met with untimely, even violent, oblivion, their scratchings considerably less permanent than the pictographs of the native Sheepeaters.

Homesteaders here were tardy, partly because the better sites elsewhere were already taken, partly because this country was so belatedly surveyed. These men wanted their own anchorhold. ("To be rooted is perhaps the most important and least recognized need of the human soul," said philosopher Simone Weil.) They came to the Middle Fork for tangled reasons—immigrants, washouts, flotsam— lodged alongside a passing thing, and pitched their hopes on the ground and the water. In elder years, health invariably proved the hardest dog to keep under the porch. Surrogates supplanted them, briefly. The West is a great place for turnover. So was the Middle Fork. With the flow of years, their names and places have worn smooth as river stones beneath a swirl of currents. Still, looking back, their efforts remain nothing short of heroic.

Following Spread:
The pink light of dawn is reflected in a clear, pristine pool at Ayers Meadow.

After scouting this site on a previous trip, I hiked
downstream from Sheepeater Camp to a rock

Sheepeater Bend outcrop jutting out 150 feet above the
river with a raptor's view both up and
down the canyon. I liked the alluring curve of the river
as it disappeared into the trees downstream, so I
metered for the reflective surface of the water,
creating the effect of a bright swatch of river cutting
through a darkened landscape.

M.L.

By A River

David Wagoner

Your choice was always clear: not the long struggle
Upstream against the current, against the constant
Headlong pummeling of snow-melt and downpour
Nor the leaf-slow easy drifting
Downstream, the way all trees on a cutbank bend
Before they fall, but simply staying
Here by the river where you watch and wait
For what appears, moves past, and vanishes.

You've learned what you can about this watery sky,
Its rearrangement of your slight reflections,
Its turmoil, each moment so subtly various,
You can hardly tell, can hardly remember
What you marveled over only a glance before:
The shimmering, the lovely formalities
Of a chaos you can touch with your finger-ends,
A surface whose tarnished and burnished galaxies
Are born and borne away, but instantly
Return in a translucent blossoming.

You know under that surface always, no matter
What may seem apparent by sunlight,
Cloudlight, or moonlight, another life is passing,
Not just the stones and snags, the common bed-load
Of all rivers, not only the star-backed swimmers
Whose falls and springs once dazzled you into believing
You could dream your way to the source, but the Other

Whose body is never still, is always turning
Away from you downriver as if to stream
To an end beyond you through the deepest channels,
And yet remains beside you, whose light is lighter
Than air, whose breath is water, whose water is light.

©1999 by David Wagoner.

Autumn colors and an October snowstorm decorate
a bend in the river near Sheepeater hot springs.

Perspectives

"What I really like about the Middle Fork River trip is the fact that it covers a hundred miles. It's an expedition! You have to carry your own supplies, boats, boxes. There is no quick rescue. People take a trip like the Middle Fork seriously.

The hot springs are one glorious thing the Middle Fork has over all those other rivers. I have boated the Middle Fork in the spring, when the weather has been cool. It's great to hike up when it is cold and rainy outside and sit in a hot tub at 102 degrees. It's surreal, really."

Steve Herring
Beaverton, OR
Two Middle Fork trips

"Putting together a river trip? It's always an epic, always challenging. It can be a daunting task, but once you have done it a couple of times you start to get the hang of it. Multi-day overnight trips are definitely the best. Boating is a great way to just get out there, away from civilization, and not hear a car, or see a road. The whole ball of wax."

Donnie Benson
Salt Lake City, UT
One Middle Fork trip

"I remember the trip as pristine and crisp, pretty and untouched, but at the same time interactive. We were taking part in the wilderness as opposed to just taking pictures of it."

Coert Voorhees
Menlo Park, CA
One Middle Fork trip

"It was my first time rowing a boat and I remember thinking, 'I had better pay attention or this river is going to kick my butt really quick.'"

John Kearney
Ketchum, ID
Two Middle Fork trips

"I look forward to the relaxation of floating down the river. I like the feeling that I am an explorer. We have all sorts of guidebooks nowadays, but even with all that information you never know how much the river will have changed. You have the feeling that you are an adventurer in the middle of nowhere."

David Levine
Colorado Springs, CO
Three Middle Fork trips

"I've heard somewhere that the Middle Fork is referred to as the crown jewel of the wild and scenic river system. Well, I don't think anyone could argue with that."

Jim Siebe
Moscow, ID
Twelve Middle Fork trips

"It's right up there with the Grand Canyon. I would rank them side by side, not one better than the other. They are different experiences. The core is that when you leave, you have been affected by the experience."

Christina King
Woodland Park, CO
Ten Middle Fork trips

"We did our trip with 18 women. It was pouring down rain when we launched and the river was at 5.5 feet. We were all apprehensive. The trip was about pulling it together and realizing that we were going to be fine. We had a fantastic sense of accomplishment when we turned the corner into the Main Salmon."

Britt Overby
Telluride, CO
One Middle Fork trip

"I have boated all over the U.S. and the world. As far as northern U.S. rivers go, the Middle Fork is without a doubt number one."

Rod Huck
Salt Lake City, UT
Three Middle Fork trips

"Sleeping—the one simple rule is that I've got to have the window of the tent next to the river so it is the first thing I see in the morning. Some people position themselves in relation to the groover or the kitchen, but I've got to be near the river. After all, it's what we came out here for."

Jim Siebe
Moscow, ID
Twelve Middle Fork trips

"One of my favorite things to do is to spin in the eddies in Impassable Canyon, and look up at the walls and wonder how long it took the rocks way up there to get down into the river itself."

Joel Mallett
Ketchum, ID
Four Middle Fork trips

"Any Middle Fork trip is really two trips: the planning of the trip, in terms of organizing food packing, shuttles, vehicles, equipment, and gear. Part two is the actual trip down the river. It's a whole lot of work before you get on the river and a whole lot of fun when you're on the river. You just forget about everything else and enjoy the history and geology and natural beauty of the experience."

Michael Malko
Hailey, ID
Twenty-three
Middle Fork trips

Dagger Falls Morning

Not normally run by commercial outfitters,
Dagger Falls requires a long portage or gutsy
run by boaters floating Marsh Creek
in early spring. After running it
ourselves on a private trip in May of 2002, we
camped just below the falls. This photo, taken
early the next morning, shows the fish ladder
(constructed in the 1950s) with the churning
power of Dagger Falls.

M.L.

When low water dictates launching trips from Indian Creek, the guides float or "dead head" the boats from Boundary Creek to Indian Creek in a single day. After enduring a day of thunder showers and rain, we all enjoyed the camaraderie of the campfire before the guests flew in the following day. The cold, clear night drew the moisture out of the canyon, and the next morning the river was enveloped in fog.

River Mist

M.L.

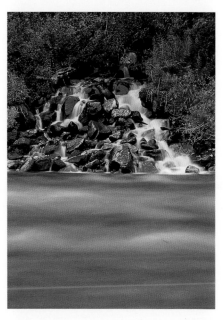

Top to Bottom:
A trio of sego lilies pushes up from a meadow floor in early spring.

Lake Creek tumbles into the swifter waters of the Middle Fork River.

Rocks coated in minerals punctuate the bubbling water of a nearby hot spring.

Opposite:
Forests of lodgepole pine and Douglas fir border a peaceful bend in the river below Sheepeater Camp at mile 13.

During the fire season of 2000, over 500,000 acres of the Frank Church Wilderness were burned by

Frank Church Fire, 2000   wildfires raging for more than two months. In October of the same year, I floated the Middle Fork with a friend to observe the effects of the fires along the river corridor. On the second day of our trip, I took this image (left) of a small stand of pines recovering from the Mortar Creek Burn of 1979—nearly twenty years previous. These new trees stood out in stark contrast to the charred forests I encountered downstream—as seen in the image above, taken up Pistol Creek near mile 21.

M.L.

On the Middle Fork Every Time is Perfect

by William Studebaker

THIS IS THE ELEVENTH TIME I've made this pilgrimage. On the fourth day, as I drift in my kayak past the mouth of Camas Creek, the desire arises to beach and walk upstream a couple hundred yards to the campsite where I spent timeless summer days as a boy. I do not, however. That perfect world is at rest, so I leave it at that.

Back in the early '50s, Dad was the alternate ranger for the Yellow Jacket Forest Service District. Dad, Mom, and I traveled by mule train to the site on Camas Creek, where we lived in a white canvas-wall tent.

Mom cooked on a Coleman stove and a campfire—pancakes, Dutch-oven bread, Spam, potatoes, sausage gravy, and an occasional pine grouse. We pulled fresh rainbow trout (maybe bull trout) from the lazy hole that swirled gently above the pack bridge spanning the creek. Or we walked a few hundred yards to the place where Camas Creek met the Middle Fork of the Salmon River, and cast our lines in the ripples where the big cutthroat trout lay.

It was easy living for me, a young boy whose parents encouraged him to roam. I could say I climbed the hills, but there were no hills. Camas and the Middle Fork are cuddled by mountains with their feet firmly planted on the shorelines. So I climbed from the foot of a mountain to the crest of a ridge, but never reached the top of a single mountain. The days were too short.

Some days we went to the hot springs above the Mormon Ranch to bathe, or the Flying B to visit, or beyond, to the Bernard Ranger Station for business. But most days, I wandered away from camp to sit on a mountainside perch in the pine duff, watching for the few boaters who came down the river, or followed a pack string snaking its way along Aparejo Point.

Back then my knowledge of the Middle Fork was limited to the stretch from the Middle Fork Lodge to Big Creek. Downriver, below the mouth of Big Creek, was Impassable Canyon. I had heard rumors about it—25 miles of rough, tough country where a boy would have to climb steep mountains and scramble over cliff faces. And, if he did, he might get lost and never be found. I knew Earl Parrott,

Opposite:
A commercial rafting guide strains on the oars to avoid the rocks at Pistol Creek Rapid near mile 21.

the man some called the hermit of Impassable Canyon. What that meant, I wasn't quite sure. Although he was a friend of the family and died in my grandparents' home, I knew little of his peculiar life, of his truck farm in the middle of nowhere. I just thought that he was an unusual man who knew his way around Impassable Canyon . . . someone I imagined I could be.

Now, my gear is tied to a raft, not a mule, and I travel with my wife, Judy, and children, Tona, Robert, Tyler, and Eric. At each camp, as the scenery changes, I take them up trails and mountainsides to view tens of thousands of acres, primeval in their capacity to permeate and shock sensibility. Soon, the kids are roaming alone, walking the trails or climbing as high as dusk will allow. I have to call them back as though they are lost. They are changed by a few hours of primitive privacy, which, in their lives, is afforded only by our chosen wilderness. There's nothing like solitude—once felt, always sought.

Opposite:
Boaters take cover in Driftwood Camp during a brief summer rainstorm.

Above:
A child explores the eddies and swimming holes of Loon Canyon.

A kayaker gets his stern squirted while running the lower section of Dagger Falls.

Walks combine with floating to form different ways of wandering. In the '50s, I sat taking snapshots with my mind. Now, I drift. The river moves along at three or four miles an hour, the scenery flowing by as in a real-life movie. The smells of the forest reach me: Doug fir and buck brush. Temperature envelops me: warm by day, cool by night. And there is touch: the splash of water and the grip of granite.

Floating the Middle Fork is a six-day reel, an immersion in experience. We began in high country, near the Sawtooth Mountains, and will end in the low country of the Salmon River (3,300 feet). It is a journey through a half-dozen ecosystems—borderline alpine and yellow pine forests, and deep, defying, arid canyons. The river is plot, set, and scenery—a stage for testing character. The whitewater and wilderness script resolves conflict. The only act for me is to be, for each of us to find ourselves.

For kayakers, the river is also a playground filled with surf waves, play holes, wave trains for countless wave wheels, and eddy lines for squirting and flat-water wheels. If I can throw the trick, there is water in which to do it. It is downstream, hunt-and-play kayaking at its best. The Middle Fork challenges rafters, too, from top to bottom, giving them reason to take powerful strokes and weave between boulders. It is a joy to maneuver successfully through rapids such as Powerhouse and Haystack, and land the line in Hancock.

These rapids are signals that we are near the end of our pilgrimage. My mind drifts back to linger at the put in, and that cold, fleecy morning when I packed a bucket of creek water back to camp, where the crew members were fixing breakfast and stirring their courage. If I could call everyone back, I would start over. I would run Dagger Falls again and get submerged in the pure water at the headwaters. But I'm not discontent. I'm just floating, daydreaming, and letting another perfect pilgrimage join the others.

Opposite:
A large granite boulder disrupts the river's flow.

The swift, confined rapids in the Upper Canyon provide thrills for rafters and photgraphers alike.

Following Spread:
Morning light reflects an open blue sky in a shadowy pool just below Ramshorn Rapid at mile 5.

Middle Canyon

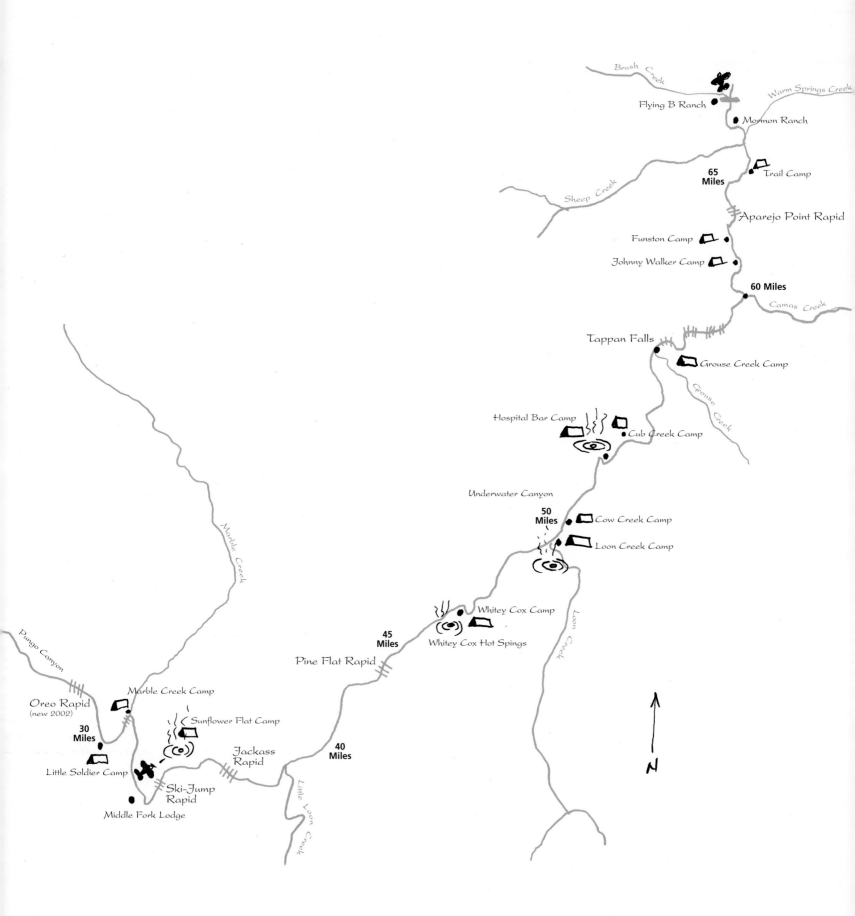

Brush Creek

Warm Springs Creek

Flying B Ranch

Mormon Ranch

65 Miles Trail Camp

Sheep Creek

Aparejo Point Rapid

Funston Camp

Johnny Walker Camp

60 Miles

Camas Creek

Tappan Falls

Grouse Creek Camp

Grouse Creek

Hospital Bar Camp

Cub Creek Camp

Underwater Canyon

50 Miles Cow Creek Camp

Loon Creek Camp

Marble Creek

Whitey Cox Camp

Whitey Cox Hot Spings

45 Miles

Loon Creek

Pine Flat Rapid

Pungo Canyon

Marble Creek Camp

Oreo Rapid
(new 2002)

Sunflower Flat Camp

30 Miles

40 Miles

Jackass Rapid

Little Soldier Camp

Ski-Jump Rapid

Little Loon Creek

Middle Fork Lodge

N

62

Middle Canyon

by William Studebaker

THE MIDDLE STRETCH OF
the Middle Fork is a Middle Earth—
an odd combination of possibilities. A
good portion of it runs along the 45th
parallel, halfway between the Equator
and the North Pole. The Middle
Stretch offers a transition between the
green, lush Upper Canyon and the
raw, primal Lower Canyon. The Middle Canyon undulates,
rolling off into purple and blue horizons. Large creeks like
Loon and Camas pour in. The geology shifts, soils appear.

And this Middle stretch is the most civilized—if you
consider a chunk of river nearly 40 miles long with a half-
dozen permanent residences civilized. These folks are gritty
characters and tenacious, and they're friendly—in their
own way.

After leaving Indian Creek, that drainage of demarca-
tion between the Upper and Middle regions of the Middle
Fork, the river continues north. In this case, north is down.
The climate changes subtly as the elevation drops and the
humidity thins. Lodgepole pines are replaced by 150-foot
Ponderosas and scattered Douglas fir. The hills carry more
bulk; the river, more water. Large side streams appeal to the
adventurous kayaker.

The Middle Fork trail widens and flattens, and so
does the river. This is the place to relax, fish, and stretch
out in the sun. You're at least two days
from Boundary Creek, maybe three
or four, depending on your mode of
travel—hoof, foot, or boat.

In this realm, reams of human
history mingle with the wild and
undaunted. Not far from here, the
great gray wolf was recently reintro-
duced to central Idaho. Now she roams, glad to be home.
If you're lucky, you'll hear her howl and yap at her pups,
calling them close, in her wolfish way.

Small houses perch on the high banks. Periodically,
ranches dot the shores. A few piles of "grubstake" cobbles
clutter the mouths of creek and freshet, offering a standing
legacy from a time when this region was explored by
miners, settled by a few hardy pioneers—or, refashioned
to their liking. And there are legacies from Native
Americans: fishing camps, pit houses, and various debutage
from stone tools.

The Middle stretch is a paradox, both passive and
rushing headlong: Pine Flat Pool, a flat, alluring deep corner, and Tappan Falls, pure exhilaration. A few other
rapids, Jackass, Tappan I, Tappan II, Tappan III, and
Aparejo Point, break up the hypnotic flow. The Middle,
from Indian Creek to the Flying B Guest Ranch, offers a
respite—a time for reflection, and also for preparation.

Foreshadowing what lies ahead, the Middle Fork carves
an underwater canyon just below Loon Creek.

Preceding Spread:
The east-west orientation of the canyon at Loon Creek
produces a spectacular light show at sunset.

The chilly waters of Loon Creek slip by the steaming waters of a natural hot spring tub.

Preceding Spread:
Kayakers enjoy the whitewater at Tappan Falls.

68

Geology of the Middle Fork

by Matt Leidecker

THE MIDDLE FORK OF THE SALMON River flows through an incredibly vast and varied canyon. The river changes drastically from the put in at Boundary Creek to its confluence with the Main Salmon, dropping 3,000 feet in the process and creating the heart-pounding rapids, rolling waves, swirling eddies, and white sand beaches that attract river runners time and time again to the canyon.

The Central Idaho mountains took 100 million years to form, but the Middle Fork has been carving into its canyon for only two of those 100 million. Within that time, glaciers have carved their way through the mountains surrounding the Middle Fork, resulting in fluctuations between erosion and deposition of rock waste in the canyon. More recently, on a time scale that humans can observe, sand bars continue to grow or shrink with seasonal runoff, gravel channels change with high water flows, and side canyons flood, depositing sediment fans into the river. Many ancient cultures believe that rocks hold the story of the earth, and the rocks along the Middle Fork recall a history of formation as vast and varied as the canyon itself.

Float boaters launching from Boundary Creek will encounter a geologic landscape disguised by a high alpine forest of Douglas fir and lodgepole pine. Outcrops of dark granite and graniodiorite punctuate the landscape and tower above the river. These broken towers and shattered abutments overlook the entrance to Powerhouse Rapid. Long open slopes of broken rock or talus are a testament to the freeze/thaw erosion that occurs during the winter months. River camps, and old miners' cabins occupy the forested terraces left behind by historical river beds, and Native American hunting blinds can be found in the rocks where the talus meets these flat benches. Sandy beaches are few and far between and many of the rapids run over bedrock ledges or through slots in the cliff walls.

Around Indian Creek, the canyon begins to open up. The geology in this region is dominated by the crumbly hillsides of the easily eroded pink granite known as the Casto pluton. Black dikes of liquid basalt that squeezed and oozed into cracks in the granite during volcanic eruptions millions of years ago, can be seen close to the water around Marble Creek Rapid. The open landscape of the Middle Canyon section accommodates larger and more expansive river terraces. Both Native Americans and early pioneers took advantage of these islands of flat landscape in the sea of mountains to establish camps, hunting grounds, and rudimentary homesteads. These flat terraces, created through the accumulation and filling of the river canyon with rock waste, now provide ideal locations for several backcountry airstrips and irrigated fields such as those encountered at

Opposite (Top to Bottom):
Streamside granite.
Footprints on a sandy bar.
Metamorphic Rock Swirl.
Cliffside Crack.
Grazing Bighorn Sheep.
Rafters in Tappan Pool.
River Rock.

the Middle Fork Lodge, Loon Creek, and the Flying B Ranch. Like the soft pink granite of this middle section of river, the rapids are equally quiet and unassuming. Pungo Canyon below Indian Creek, and Tappan Canyon above the Flying B provide the only significant whitewater. These sections, not surprisingly, cut through and expose more resistant metamorphic rocks, which were molded like silly putty by intense pressure and temperatures deep in the earth's crust. Boaters scouting the Class IV Tappan Falls should take notice of this beautifully sculpted stone.

Almost immediately below the Flying B Ranch, the river enters the lower canyon. It is here that the geology shines brightest. The desert climate supports relatively sparse vegetation and massive vertical expanses of rock are laid open like a book. A complicated mix of disfigured sedimentary rock and intrusive granite dominates the river between Haystack Rapid and Waterfall Creek. Liquid intrusions, originating from the pink granite of the middle canyon, were injected into the broken mountains downstream. A tortured fold of quartzite juts vertically into the air just below Rattlesnake Cave on river left, testimony to the powerful forces of colliding tectonic plates involved in building these mountains. Near Waterfall Creek, the river slices through a massive expanse of light, salt-and-pepper granite known as the Idaho Batholith. For several miles, the scenery is dominated by these massive granite walls before giving way to the twists and striations of metamorphic gneiss, which continues to the confluence with the Main Salmon. In this deep river canyon, relatively few river terraces have been preserved. Boaters, like the Native Americans before them, take advantage of the large sand and gravel bars for camping along the river.

It is an amazing geology—a landscape of dark sedimentary rocks twisted by heat and pressure, of open, rolling hillsides and sheer cliff faces carved out of granite and punctuated by crescent beaches of fine, honey-colored sand. Recorded here are major geologic events such as a mighty collision between North America and the Pacific Ocean plate, the end of the last Ice Age and the fall of massive glaciers, and the erosive force and power of wind and rain and water—an ancient narrative of the land.

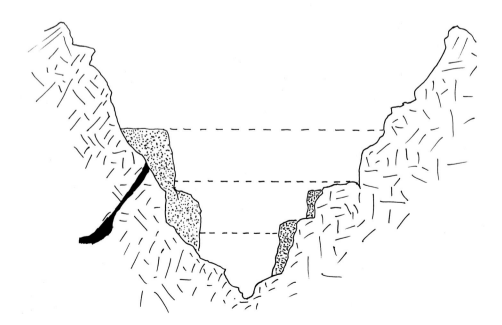

A hypothetical cross section of the Middle Fork Canyon shows various levels of river terraces. During historical ice ages, the canyons filled with rock waste resulting in broad, flat, braided river channels similar to modern day rivers emanating from glacial tongues in Alaska. When the mountainous glaciers receded, the Middle Fork River incised and eroded laterally, removing all but these remnant terrace surfaces. Each major terrace surface may be linked to historical glacial episodes that occured roughly every 100,000 years.

An example of the powerful forces of river hydraulics can be witnessed in the new rapid created at this bend near mile 28.

River Hydraulics-Oreo Rapid In July 2002, an intense thunderstorm caused a sudden landslide down Orleano Creek in Pungo Canyon. The resulting debris fan nearly dammed the river, pinching it into a narrow channel on river left and depositing a large amount of rock and log debris, resulting in a new Class III rapid. Dubbed "Oreo," this new rapid will change drastically next spring as the force of high water washes the logs and smaller sediment downstream.

If you owned land in Western Idaho roughly 100 million years ago, you had oceanfront property. The landmass that is now Central Idaho was a relatively flat lowland plain of sedimentary deposits on the margin between ocean and continent. The ceaseless shifting on the earth's surface eventually resulted in the Pacific Ocean plate subducting underneath Idaho and North America. The Pacific plate continued to dive and melt, carrying rafted pieces of continental crust—much like the Hawaiian Islands—into the subduction zone at the edge of Western Idaho. This resulted in a terrific collision that rippled across what is now Idaho, Montana, and Wyoming, reaching as far north as Canada and south towards Mexico to create the infant stages of the great and vast Rocky Mountains.

To the west, much of the sedimentary rock that dominated Central Idaho was folded, twisted, and faulted into unrecognizable metamorphic rock. These are very likely the same rocks exposed in Tappan Canyon, as well as the last ten miles of Impassable Canyon. To the east, many of these sedimentary layers slid off the top of the rising bubble of igneous granite known as the Idaho Batholith and piled into the Bitterroot, White Clouds, Lost River, and Lemhi ranges. Eventually the Pacific plate broke at the new western edge of the North American continent (roughly Central Oregon) and began subducting again. For more than 95 million years, this process continued, marked by massive earthquakes, faulting in mountain ranges, and intrusions of liquid magma from deep beneath

the surface, creating the mountains of Central Idaho, and then the ranges of the Northwest, the Rockies, northern Sierras, and Cascades.

As the geologic time scale began to compress and the rise and fall of mountains slowed to an intangible pace, the history of the Middle Fork River began. Roughly two million years ago the river was confined in its present day canyon. The forces of plate tectonics were responsible for the shape of the canyon and the bedrock geology of the surrounding mountains—the Casto pluton, Idaho Batholith granites, metamorphic and sedimentary rocks, and intrusions of molten dikes throughout the mountains of the region. During the past two million years, however, the catastrophic force of shifting plates has had little to do with the deep canyons, open terraces, and powerful rapids of the Middle Fork River Canyon. The landscape has been almost entirely shaped through the constant force of erosion and water—a process known to geologists as geomorphology.

Water falling from the sky contains energy that has the ability to shape and mold the earth. It seeps into cracks, then freezes and thaws—literally prying solid rocks from mountaintops. It accumulates in glaciers, creeping downhill and rasping the valley floors, transporting tons of sediment into river valleys. Individual raindrops act as miniature hammers, methodically chipping away at the smallest fragments of soil, as well as solid rock. But it is when these drops merge together into rivers that water has the greatest ability to carve its signature into the earth's surface. The intricate, web-like network of river drainages across our nation are the highways in which the broken pieces of mountains are tumbled, sifted, ground, and eventually transported to the oceans.

The waters confined within the canyon walls of the Middle Fork are constantly at work on the landscape. The hydraulic action of moving water is able to dislodge and transport fine-grained sediment downstream. In the springtime, churning sand and silt-laden waters tumble boulders in the river bed, acting as an abrasive which continues to grind deeper into the canyon. The river is constantly transporting and shifting its sediment load of silt, boulders, gravels, and sand and re-depositing them along the channel where river runners can observe the seasonal changes in the form of gravel bars or the fine sand beaches at Elk and Otter Bar—the result of boulders ground down by hundreds of years of river current.

It is a humbling experience to watch a river in flood and listen as the power of the water tumbles and grinds these boulders along the bottom, shifting gravel bars and rearranging entire river channels.

Most river runners love to peruse the banks and gravel bars of the Middle Fork. The tumbled stones come from all corners of the drainage basin and represent a variety of rock types spanning thousands—even millions—of years of geologic time. Some might be fascinated by the ability of the river to change the shape of its banks and bars on a seasonal basis. Others might be looking for glimpses into the geologic past when plate tectonics ruled, mountains were built, and molten rock cooled into stone. Still others might be looking for that "diamond in the rough," the perfect rock created by plate tectonics eons ago and then beautifully shaped and polished by moving water. When they pick it up and hold it in their hands there is a true merging of the geologic with the human scale of time.

Following Spread:
Thousands of years of erosion have smoothed and polished the granite bedrock of Loon Creek.

Stateland Sunset Because the sun drops below the tops of mountain peaks well before it paints the sky with color, boaters rarely see spectacular sunsets from the bottom of the Middle Fork Canyon. Breathtaking sunsets such as this image taken from Stateland Right Camp, are more frequently seen in the open areas of the river. I wanted to highlight the silhouette of the ponderosa trees across the river, so I experimented, metering off the bright sky and composing the image with the river in the foreground to give depth to the scene.

M.L.

Opposite:
A billowing thunderhead high above the Middle Fork radiates the light of the setting sun.

FIRE BY THE RIVER
David Wagoner

We gather wood, the bleached, clay-covered branches
As heavy as fossils, drag them to the shore,
      And cross them, touching a match
To a nest of twigs. And the fire begins between us
Under this evening kindled by our breath.

It gathers dusk in tight against our backs,
Lighting us half by half. The river roars
      Like a fire drawn through a valley.
The smoke pours down to the water's edge like a creek
And empties into the broad, downstreaming night.

The first chill draws our arms around each other.
Like firelight under eyelids, the stars spread out.
      We lie down with ourselves.
The lighted halves of our bodies sink together.
The moon leans inward, banking on darkness.

Set free by our sleep and coming down to the water,
The bears, the deer, the martens dark as their fur,
      As soundless as night herons,
All drink and turn away, making no light.
The tail of the wind is stirring the soft ashes,

And nothing of ours will be left in the morning
Though we guard it now through dewfall and ground mist.
      But here at the heart of night
A salmon leaps: the smack of his wild body
Breaks through the valley, splashing our sleep with fire.

© 1999 by David Wagoner.

Opposite:
The perfect Middle Fork moment—a campfire
beneath the Milky Way.

Following Spread:
Red rocks, green moss, and whitewater—Bear
Creek as it tumbles into the Middle Fork near
mile 62.

Perspectives

"No matter how hot the weather, no matter how difficult the situation, at the end of the day when you lie down on your bed and look up at the stars, you realize that it is all worthwhile."

Larry McGowen
Thirty-three seasons

"Of all the rivers I've run, whether in New Zealand or anywhere else, none changes as much as the Middle Fork. Even the Grand Canyon is pretty much the same when you put on compared with where you take out, but the Middle Fork is constantly evolving, all the way down."

Matt Jost
Nine seasons

"The best thing in the 100 miles is the fact that you can start in a high alpine setting with lodgepole pines and move through ponderosa forests, high-desert sage, then finish in that spectacular granite gorge.

Since it's a free-flowing river, you can't memorize lines but have to read water and run as you go. The river is constantly changing: Rocks get shifted around and high water brings in new logs. And not many trips drop 3,000 feet in their duration. You combine all of those things and you have a pretty amazing river."

Eric Rector
Fourteen seasons

"It gets into your skin, into your blood. It's an addiction—a good addiction, but still an addiction. You want to go back and you will. I got to a junction in my life about twelve years ago where I realized that I didn't want to quit. I knew I couldn't make a great living guiding, but I didn't want to pound nails or anything else. So I went back to school and got my teaching degree so I could guide. It's what I am and something that I'm proud of. It's directed my life, shaped it."

Deano Snell
Twenty-nine seasons

"I'm kind of homeless, really. As far as home goes, I've got a storage unit and three P.O. boxes."

Dave Verner
Fifteen seasons

"I always joke with my fellow guides that we live in this fairy-tale land called Idaho, where we go into this amazing wilderness and people actually pay us to take them down a river."

Matt Jost
Nine seasons

"Working on the Middle Fork was the first time I ever experienced an almost complete sense of contentment. Waking up in the morning and knowing you are doing exactly what you want to be doing, exactly where you want to be doing it. It's an empowering realization to have at such a young age."

Jim Norton
Nine seasons

"It's hard to summarize fifty-some years of boating in just one paragraph. It's been a fantastic experience to run and see the river develop."

Dave Helfrich
Fifty-four seasons

"We all get a kick out of the rapids, otherwise we probably wouldn't be there. Running a flat river with no white-water would be a lot like driving a city bus—just doesn't seem that exciting."

Don Wouda
Thirty-two seasons

"The river teaches me about commitment, about making quick decisions and reacting to them. It teaches me about awareness, paying attention, reading subtleties, and listening to myself. You always have to remember that the river is the master."

Jessica Cortright
Five seasons

"The Middle Fork has a wonderful way of making you feel small. Never insignificant, but small, like a piece of something vast and orderly. The Middle Fork will take an inflated ego and deflate it back to its natural state within the first ten minutes on the water."

Tim Akapah
Seven seasons

"I love it. It's my favorite place on earth! It makes me who I am."

Stephanie Bernt
Five seasons

"Among an awful lot of memories, all of them good, probably the best is being able to work with my son on the Middle Fork."

Gaynor Goth
Thirty-three seasons

Only once in twelve seasons of guiding have I had
the opportunity to camp at Loon Creek during a full

Full Moon Over Loon Creek   moon. After a talkative evening
by the campfire, a few of the
guides headed up to the hot springs for a relaxing
soak. I stopped on the bridge and set up my tripod
to make this four-minute moonlit exposure of Loon
Creek before heading up to join the others.

M.L.

Every year our schedule coincides with Schaefer's
Guide Service. These drift boat guides from Oregon

McKenzie Boats specialize in fishing trips down the Middle
Fork. The metal or wooden-hulled boats
are delicate, very maneuverable, and perfect for fly
fishing. I awoke early one morning at the Indian Creek
campsite to capture this thirty-second exposure of a
line of gently rocking boats shrouded in early morning
river mist.

M.L.

Left to Right (From Top):
Kayaks drying out.
Dutch oven cooking.
Daybreak at Loon Creek.
Queing up for the hole at Pine Flat Rapid.
Punching the wave in Tappan Falls.

Opposite: A darkened hillside of red ninebark changing colors with the coming fall season at Johnny Walker Camp near mile 60.

Johnny Walker

Above: An aerial view of the same canyon shows Johnny Walker Camp and the line etchings of higher river terraces, both upstream and downstream.

M.L.

Kayaking the Middle Fork Tributaries: Al, John, and the Old Days

by Greg Moore

ALTHOUGH THE MIDDLE FORK remains remarkably pristine considering the number of floaters it transports each year, the river's popularity has brought with it an inevitable sense of encroaching civilization. During prime season, the put in at Boundary Creek can be a circus, the good camps are all taken, and it seems as if there's another boating party around every bend. Luckily, however, there are places nearby where you can still boat the old way, places where you pack all your gear into your kayak and just go—no rafts to haul around, no lawn chairs, no gas-fired grills, no coolers. Just the basics.

You can camp where you want and have the river to yourself on the Middle Fork's three biggest tributaries—Big Creek, Loon Creek, and Camas Creek. Loon enters from the east about halfway down the river; Camas farther down from the same side; and Big Creek flows in from the west still farther down, just above Impassable Canyon.

The first known run of Loon Creek by white men was in 1980 by two Sun Valley-area residents, Al Reynolds and John Ward. The two have since run at least one of the creeks every year. Pioneers of Idaho boating, they're now in their late fifties. They've lost some hair and some muscle tone, but remain strong paddlers.

Back then it was a different world. If you saw a car coming down the highway with a kayak on the rack, you stopped to see who it was and where they were boating.

"In the old days," Al says, "the boats were made of glass and the men were made of steel. You used to boat Saturday and Sunday and fix the dings from Monday through Thursday."

John moved to Ketchum in 1971, after a teaching stint in California, to become a partner in Natural Progression Kayaks. The company built glass boats in a small shop on Sun Valley Road that now houses an auto parts store.

"I was the fiberglass guy, killing brain cells," laughs John. "I've always wanted to go into the auto parts store and ask those guys if they itch when they go home."

The owners of Natural Progression went into business by borrowing a friend's Lettmann Mark IV kayak and surreptitiously cutting off the cockpit combing to form a mold around the hull. When they were done, they glued the combing back on and thanked their friend for the loan, saying, yes, they had enjoyed their river trip. They changed the mold just enough to avoid a lawsuit, but got sued anyway. The suit dragged on until it eventually ran out of steam. The company was sold to a paddler in Salmon in 1977 and renamed Salmon River Boatworks. By then, the plastic holloform kayak had been introduced, and the writing was on the wall for fiberglass boats.

Opposite:
Large boulders at Loon Creek exposed during low water conditions.

Left to Right:
Camping along the river.
A colorful palette of flowers and lichen.
Remnants of a burn nearly hidden by brilliant
green grass.

One recent sunny day in June, I left Ketchum to run Loon Creek with Al, John, and two other paddlers. We planned to spend two days on the creek, then hook up with a raft trip to be legal on the two-day float down the lower half of the Middle Fork. It was a routine pilgrimage for Al and John, but I had only done the creek once, years before. It felt new to me.

We left the highway at Sunbeam northeast of Stanley, and drove up a dirt road along the Yankee Fork. On the way to Loon Creek summit, we passed by the dilapidated remains of the 19th-century mining town of Bonanza; the lifeless landscape created by a monster gold dredge in the 1940s; and the still-operating Grouse Creek mine—a huge, fresh scrape on the mountainside to the west. After a fine view of the White Clouds Mountains from the summit, we bounced and slid and rattled our way down the road along Jordan Creek.

Two hours, one flat tire, and one bent muffler later, we arrived at the put in, shut down the engines, and let the dust settle. All was quiet, save the soft rippling of the creek.

We yanked the boats off the rack, dropping them with a thud on the dirt, and pulled our gear out of the cars onto the ground. We stuffed clothes and sleeping bags and food into our stow floats until there was nothing left lying on the grass, then said good-bye to the shuttle drivers and dragged the boats to the creek.

Al donned the white hockey helmet he's boated in for decades—old school, and proud of it. We snapped spray skirts over the cockpit lips, dipped our paddles into the glassy water of the eddy, and pulled into the current.

Downstream at last.

The creek wound between steep hillsides spotted with Douglas fir and arrowleaf balsamroot with big yellow flowers in full bloom. Perfume from thousands of white syringa blossoms wafted to midstream. Dark, weathered granite towers rose above us like witches' castles.

The party spread out as we negotiated the mostly Class III rapids. Running a small creek can be a more active experience than running a big river, if you want it to be. Eddies—playful little eddies with blue pools—beckoned from both sides of the creek, inviting me to come on in and swirl around for a while. I fell behind the rest of the group as I ferried back and forth, zipping into each eddy, then cranking a duffek stroke as I looked downstream toward my next play spot.

Creek running isn't without its hazards, however. Narrow streams provide a multitude of spots where logs can get jammed from bank to bank. Logs are dangerous because the water flows both over and under them, without the pillow of backwash that forms against a rock, so a kayak is likely to pin, or even wrap, if it bangs into one. Branches make it even worse. We encountered several logs that first afternoon on Loon Creek. Some we could slide under, others we could barely squeeze by. Only twice did we have to portage.

Then, as three of us were floating down the middle of the creek, chatting and not paying too much attention, we realized we were quickly approaching a downed tree that extended about three quarters of the way across from the left bank. Two of us spun quickly and made it around the right side, but John, who was farthest out to midstream, didn't have time. His boat slammed up against the log and flipped upstream. He kept his cool, though, and, while upside down, shoved off the bottom of the river with his paddle until he pushed his boat around the end of the log. It was a much smarter move than rolling up and risking getting pinned.

We stopped to camp at a meadow where horse packers had left a fire grate. A kayak, even an old-style one, doesn't have much room inside. As we unloaded, we pulled out the smallest items of camp gear offered by modern technology—compact sleeping bags, bivy sacks or tarps, tiny headlamps, and quick-cooking packets of food.

After dinner, Al reached into his boat and pulled out his Flexi-flask (patent pending), bulging with a load of Scotch. I perked up to see it, not because I wanted any, but because I knew that once the cap was unscrewed, river stories would start flowing. "Might as well lighten the load," Al said, tipping the flask to his mouth.

It didn't take long. The reminiscences began with a comment from John about the days when river running was deemed more important than earning much of a living, and when Al had weaned a long-ago girlfriend "from good Scotch to cheap wine."

Then there was "Space" (so named because he saved on rent by living in someone's crawl space), who liked to boat "on the natural" and subsisted primarily on avocados and bean sprouts. In keeping with his "the-lighter-the-better" theory of expeditionary boating, Space eschewed tent and sleeping bag. On the first night of a Middle Fork trip with John and Al, he went to bed in his wetsuit, burying himself up to his neck in the sand. The warmth stored in the beach faded, of course, soon after the sun went down. Having learned his lesson, the next night Space dragged every piece of flammable wood he could find to his sleeping spot to build a bonfire so huge, Al said, "you woke up in the middle of the night and it was like the middle of the day." Space would set his conflagration once each night, sprawl out at a comfortable distance, and roll toward it as it shrank.

Al and John spoke, too, of the "ghost boater of the river," a local kayaker named Harold who went even lighter on food than Space. His modus operandi was to mooch off other parties as he went downstream. One day, Al said, a friend approached him on the street and ranted about "this guy with wild blue eyes" who had showed up at dinnertime at the put in to deliver a frenzied monologue while helping himself to a lengthy meal. The next morning, he took off down the river without a permit. The Forest Service soon spotted him, and radio messages were dispatched downstream. A manhunt was launched. Accustomed to the five-day schedule of the average raft trip, however, the rangers underestimated Harold's paddling strength. On that trip, he ran the entire 100 miles of the Middle Fork in one day. "The Forest Service never caught up to him," Al said. "They looked for four days. By that time he was long gone and on his next trip."

In the old days money was scarce, and the boaters' outdoor gear showed it. Army surplus sleeping bags were popular. One model had a high-tech, quick-release zipper mechanism that allowed the user to jump out and confront the enemy on a moment's notice. Al and his friend, Mike, were using those bags on a river trip in Montana when Al woke one morning to see two grizzly cubs sniffing about camp. He knew mama bear couldn't be far behind. "Psst, Mike!" Al whispered. "Grizzlies!" Mike stuck his head out of his bag and yanked on the quick-release mechanism. It didn't work. Mike began to panic.

"He was writhing around on the ground like some huge, khaki worm," Al laughed. As Al was preparing to run and leave Mike to his fate, mama bear grunted and the cubs took off into the woods.

The stories flowed on, swirling in eddies of monologue and drifting forward as each memory pushed a new one to the surface. I was starting to yawn, though, and left for bed as the fire turned to glowing coals.

When I woke, a band of sunshine was dropping down the fir-covered hillside across the river. One more half-day to the confluence with the Middle Fork.

About noon, we stopped at the Bennett Creek pack bridge to scout Loon Creek's final gorge, which holds its most difficult whitewater. We walked down the trail about 100 feet above the river, peering at the succession of steep drops. We saw one log that would require a quick portage. Just upstream was an abrupt, six-foot drop, partly hidden by an overhanging cliff—the crux of the gorge.

"Yeah, it's runnable," Al said. "Trust me."

We did, and it was—although we all got shoved up under the cliff, our paddles scraping on the rock as we fought to get back into the current.

A mile below the gorge is Loon Creek hot springs, perhaps the Middle Fork's finest, and a popular rest stop for raft parties. Al and another member of the party took off ahead and found the pool crowded with a commercial rafting party. We enjoyed soaking and chatting with the rafters before paddling the last half-mile to the confluence.

Flowing by in rhythmic undulations, the Middle Fork looked like a big, broad river compared to Loon Creek. Fifteen rafts were tied at the confluence, and eight kayaks were stacked on the beach. The raft guides had set up about a dozen tents, and a noisy Frisbee game was taking place on the grass. It was a different world.

A trio of boats glides through Marble Creek Pool.

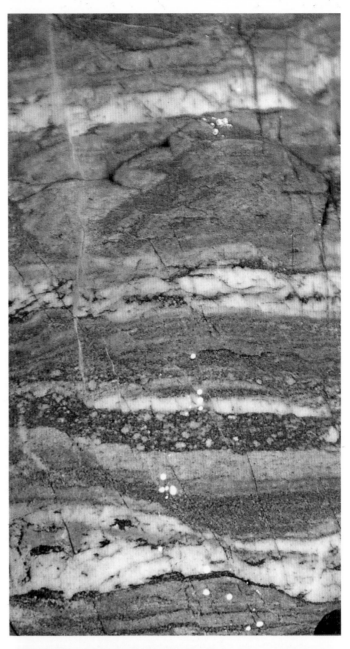
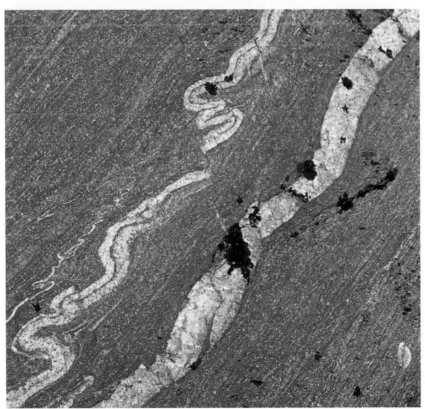
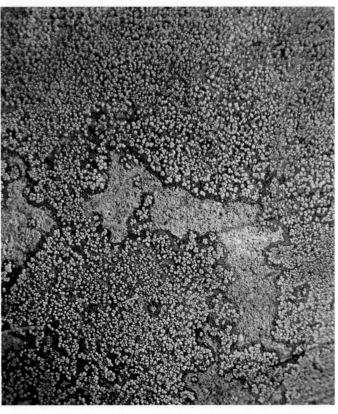

A fall morning panoramic from the upstream end of Upper Grouse Camp as the river pours into a broad pool before disappearing around the corner.

Following Spread:
A passing afternoon thunderstorm bursts forth into a majestic double rainbow over the mouth of Loon Creek Canyon.

Lower Canyon

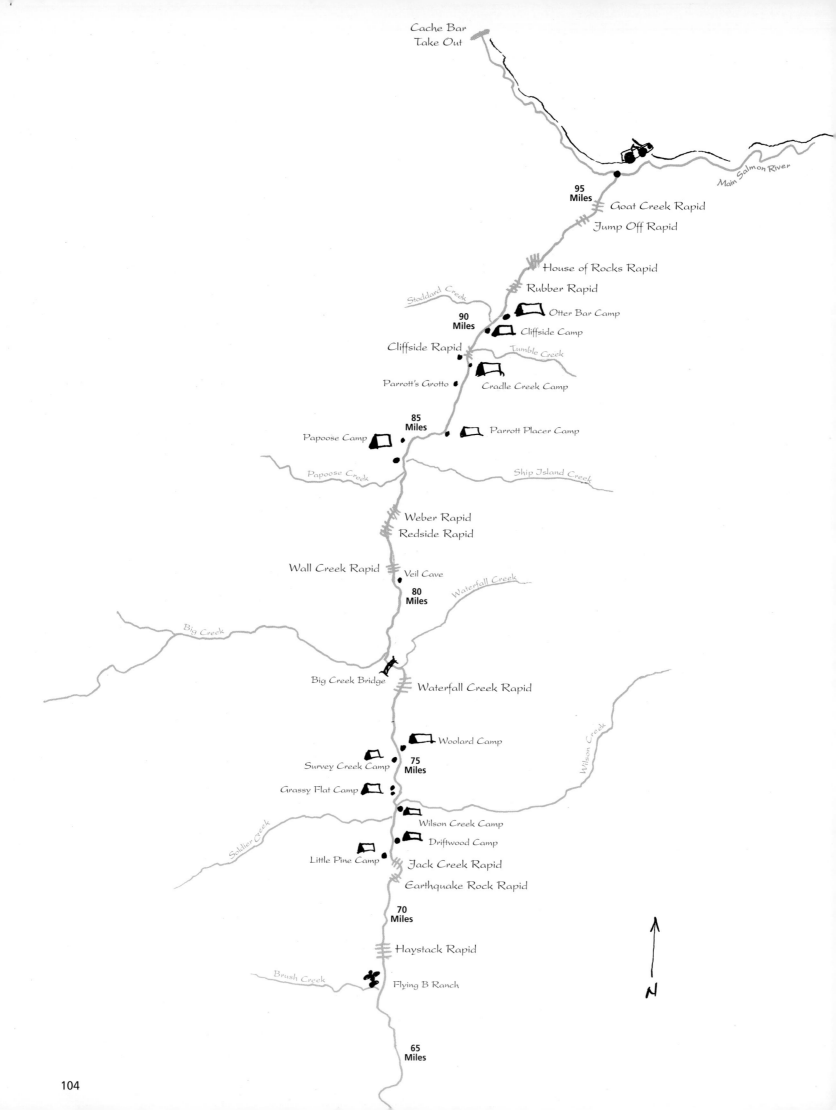

Cache Bar
Take Out

Main Salmon River

95
Miles

Goat Creek Rapid

Jump Off Rapid

House of Rocks Rapid

Rubber Rapid

Stoddard Creek

Otter Bar Camp

90
Miles

Cliffside Camp

Cliffside Rapid

Tumble Creek

Parrott's Grotto

Cradle Creek Camp

85
Miles

Papoose Camp

Parrott Placer Camp

Papoose Creek

Ship Island Creek

Weber Rapid

Redside Rapid

Wall Creek Rapid

Veil Cave

Waterfall Creek

80
Miles

Big Creek

Big Creek Bridge

Waterfall Creek Rapid

Wilson Creek

Woolard Camp

Survey Creek Camp

75
Miles

Grassy Flat Camp

Wilson Creek Camp

Soldier Creek

Driftwood Camp

Little Pine Camp

Jack Creek Rapid

Earthquake Rock Rapid

70
Miles

Haystack Rapid

Brush Creek

Flying B Ranch

N

65
Miles

Lower Canyon

by William Studebaker

AS THE RIVER GATHERS for its final stretch, a whitewater hustle similar to the one on the Upper is about to begin—but bigger this time. At Haystack Rapid, the Flying B recedes, the Middle section lets go, and the Lower descent begins in a rush.

Elk and deer are replaced by bighorn sheep and the elusive white mountain goat. Cutthroat trout mingle with rainbows. Rocks sprout into boulders, boulders into cliffs, and the earth pulls in for easy and fresh review. Buck brush, sagebrush, odd and stray Idaho fescue, and an assortment of sunflowers scent the air. Accents of Native American rock art appear here and there—simple in color, beautiful in execution.

The dominant crumbling granite of the Upper and Middle sections is interrupted by larger intrusions of the Idaho Batholith, some of the oldest rock in the world. There are excellent granite faces, chimneys, and splayed faults for those inspired to climb.

The Middle Fork trail abandons the river at Big Creek, where Impassable Canyon begins. The boat is the only way down this most athletic stretch of the Middle Fork of the Salmon River.

Imagine negotiating this canyon without help and you will understand the true meaning of wilderness. Powerful sections of water—Veil Falls, Redside Rapid, Parrott's Grotto, Lower Cliffside Rapid, and Rubber Rapid—stamp imprints on the mind. In memory, they may stream out in random beauty; but on the river, they arrive in swift succession. Hunker down: This is a hit of Western outback.

After six or seven days, maybe eight, you are wilderness-wise and feel you could spend another half-dozen days listening to Waterfall Creek, Papoose Creek, or Goat Creek. At night, you don't have to watch or listen or labor. The stars do their dance—with you.

The Lower stretch is the most private. Beauty is close and speaks to the heart. Voices echo here, coming back as you run through the new litany of places you've passed through: Boundary Creek, Velvet Falls, Tappan Falls, Flying B, House of Rocks, Hancock. Every ride comes to an end, and this one is signaled by Jump Off and Goat Creek Rapids.

But you'll be back someday. Once wild, always free—like the Middle Fork of the Salmon River.

Granite walls rising directly from the river enclose Impassable Canyon, making this stretch of the Middle Fork navigable only by water.

Preceding Spread:
The colors of a sunset reflect long veins of pink magma in the mountain below Little Pine Camp.

Following Spread:
A kayaker stands frozen in the midst of the biggest wave in Cliffside Rapid.

One afternoon while fishing up Big Creek, the guides and I watched the water change

Chalky Water from clear to glacial blue to a chalky white. That evening, while camped at Elk Bar, I hiked above the river to capture an image of the canyon as the water was running the pale, velvety white of milk.

M.L.

The Tukuduka of the Middle Fork Country

by Erik Liedecker

ON THE MORNING OF OCTOBER 1, 1879, near the confluence of Big Creek with the Middle Fork of the Salmon River, thirty-two Sheepeater Indians surrendered to Lieutenant Edward Farrow, 21st Infantry, and Lieutenant William Brown, 1st Cavalry, U.S. Army. With snow on the ground and six hundred pounds of their winter meat stores already captured, the Sheepeaters could no longer elude their more powerful, albeit more clumsy, pursuers. The costly and fiasco-ridden four-month campaign to rout the Sheepeaters from their central Idaho homeland was drawing to a close. Although reports suggest that many Sheepeaters avoided capture and continued to live in the Salmon River Mountains, the autumn of 1879 marked the beginning of the end for a people that had inhabited the Middle Fork country for over eight thousand years.

The name Sheepeater was given to the native people of Shoshone descent who inhabited the central Idaho mountains by the miners, trappers, and settlers who first encountered them—also known more generally as the Northern Shoshone. The Shoshone themselves referred to each other depending on what various bands or groups of people were doing at any given time to procure food— thus "Tukuduka" or "mountain sheep eater." Groups fishing for salmon were called "salmon eaters." Groups gathering camas were "root eaters." Although the Anglo term Sheepeater refers to a specific faction of people belonging to the Shoshone tribe, the Tukuduka, and all the Shoshone for that matter, went by different names based on their seasonal, migratory food-gathering cycle. In general, the Shoshone call themselves "newe," or "the people," and their oral history describes a homeland that extends from northern Saskatchewan to New Mexico and west to the Pacific Ocean. The Tukuduka inhabited the Salmon River Mountains, as well as the Clearwater Basin, and ranged as far west as the Blue Mountains in Oregon.

The general vicinity of the Snake River Plain was a rich and diverse geographic region. Salmon returned from the ocean to spawn in the great rivers. Roots such as camas grew plentifully on the high prairies. Buffalo thrived in enormous herds in Wyoming and Montana, and deer, elk, bear, antelope, and mountain sheep populated the mountains of central Idaho. As a result of the wildlife and topography of the Middle Fork drainage, three distinct sustenance traditions merged and influenced the development of Northern Shoshone culture. These included the seed, pine nut, and wild wheat gathering typical of Great Basin cultures; the root collecting and salmon fishing typical of Northwest cultures; and the big game hunting typical of the first humans in North America. The Shoshone appropriately developed a seasonal, migratory food-gathering cycle that included root gathering, salmon fishing, and hunting.

Opposite:
Sacred Native American pictographs dating back 8,000 years.

The introduction of horses from the Comanche people during the early eighteenth century gave the Shoshone increased mobility and made them more effective hunters. A typical migratory pattern for many Shoshone began in the spring, when various bands traveled to the Camas Prairie near present-day Fairfield to dig camas bulbs. They continued on to the Boise area for salmon fishing on the Snake and Boise Rivers. In late summer they returned to Fort Hall (the site of the modern-day reservation near Pocatello, Idaho) to graze their horses in anticipation of the fall buffalo hunts in Montana and Wyoming. To pass the winter, the Shoshone chose locales with mild weather, plentiful game, good water, and adequate forage. Some of the more consistent winter camps included the Weiser and Boise River Valleys, as well as the Baker Valley in Oregon and the Yellowstone River Valley in Montana.

Although the Tukuduka knew where to get horses in case they needed to travel long distances, they adopted them to a lesser extent than did other Shoshone people. Some experts attribute the rejection of the horse to the fact that the Tukuduka were somewhat isolated from their neighbors on the Snake River Plain. Another reason is the rugged terrain of the Tukuduka homeland: The Salmon River Mountains offer little in the way of reliable forage and are often more conducive to foot travel. Indeed, during the aforementioned Sheepeater Campaign of 1879, commanding officer Captain Reuben Bernard's troops lost over sixty head of stock between June 1 and August 26. Early trappers and miners considered the absence of horses a defining characteristic of the Tukuduka, and usually concluded that if Indians were on horses, they probably were not Sheepeaters.

Another defining characteristic of the Tukuduka was their prowess as hunters. Unlike the Snake River Plain bands, who depended on a more diverse foraging diet that included camas bulbs and, often, insects and grasshoppers, the Tukuduka were predominantly hunters and meat eaters. Tukuduka hunted elk, deer, and mountain sheep in parties of two to three men. They stalked their prey with bows and arrows fashioned from mountain sheep horns, or ambushed them from hunting blinds, many of which can still be seen along the Middle Fork corridor. To supplement their meat-based diet, the Tukuduka gathered camas roots and seeds from limber pines.

Archeological and anthropological experts have theorized a basic picture of Tukuduka life: They built conical pole lodges thatched with grass or bark. For clothing they made gowns, breachcloths, and moccasins from the hides of mountain sheep, elk, badger, deer, and rabbit. They used fur from coyotes, foxes, snowshoe rabbits, and wolves to make winter caps, headbands, robes, and blankets. With the extended family as the fundamental unit of Tukuduka social and tribal organization, monogamy was most common but plural marriage was not discouraged. Spiritual life consisted of having a guardian spirit gleaned from visions during adolescence. Almost anything from the natural world could qualify as a guardian spirit, but powerful icons included the eagle, buffalo, wolf, rattlesnake, bear, and beaver. A personal song that told the story of the guardian spirit and its protectorate was another mainstay of Tukuduka spiritual life.

By the 1860s, miners and prospectors were penetrating deeper into the traditional mountain strongholds of the Tukuduka. As was the case throughout the United States, when white enterprise encroached upon traditional Native American homelands, conflict was inevitable. Shoshone oral history recalls several instances when hostile white settlers or trappers attacked groups of natives. In fact, many Native Americans and historians believe that America's policy of Manifest Destiny called for the outright eradication of indigenous peoples. At the very least, the United States military establishment looked for any excuse to engage the armed forces.

For the Tukuduka, that excuse came in the winter of 1879 when five Chinese miners in the small town of Oro Grande on Loon Creek were murdered. Although there was never evidence to substantiate the claim, the Tukuduka were blamed for their deaths. Furthermore, the U.S. Army believed that a group of Bannocks, who had been fighting to protect the Camas Prairie from the infringement of white ranchers, had taken refuge with the Tukuduka. As a result, Brigadier General O.O. Howard dispatched Troop G, First Cavalry, commanded by Captain Reuben Bernard, to "ascertain who the murderers were; and, if Indians, to apprehend them, and bring them to Boise."

The campaign that followed lasted into the fall and was more a game of hide-and-seek than a series of military battles. The Tukuduka proved elusive foes, and twice ambushed Bernard's troops in the Big Creek drainage—once on July

29 and again on August 20. In the August attack, Private Harry Egan was shot through both legs. The company doctor amputated one limb, but Egan died despite his efforts and a marker was erected in his honor on Soldier Bar in Big Creek. A few days after Egan's death, Captain Bernard's command, out of supplies and generally exhausted, returned to Boise to regroup and re-supply. Lieutenants Brown and Farrow resumed pursuit of the Sheepeaters a third time in Big Creek, and ultimately oversaw the surrender of some Tukuduka and the end of the campaign.

One of the lessons of the Sheepeater War was an understanding of the breadth of the terrain inhabited by the Tukuduka. During the campaign, Captain Bernard's men marched nearly twelve hundred miles and endured the hardships of mountain travel, including illness, mosquitoes, hunger, deep snow, steep mountains, rocky trails, intense heat, violent thundershowers, and summer snow-storms. A final report from General Howard notes that "there is not a rougher or more difficult country for campaigning in America." Then, as now, the Salmon River Mountains—the present-day Frank Church River of No Return Wilderness—comprise some of the most rugged country in the West. That the Tukuduka made this country their home—and lived more luxuriously, some say, than their Snake River Plain counterparts—is testament to their unique relationship with their wilderness surroundings.

The end result of the campaign, however, was that most of the Tukuduka were rounded up and sent to the Fort Hall reservation near Pocatello. They were not allowed to leave without a special permit, and it wasn't until the 1930s that Shoshone people on the reservation could return to the country they considered their homeland.

Meanwhile, adventurers and explorers first started running the canyon of the Middle Fork in wooden boats and canoes. Commercial guiding on the Middle Fork was born in 1946, and in 1990 nearly 10,000 people floated through the canyon. Lionel Boyer, a Shoshone whose grandparents were among those expelled from the central Idaho mountains after the Sheepeater War, says about the people who float the river today: "What they're observing was taken away from the people who were there before."

Boyer is a 67-year-old retiree from nine terms on the Shoshone-Bannock Tribal Council. During his tenure, he interacted with various federal and state land managers on the subjects of fisheries and tribal rights. To Boyer's way of thinking, the people who now have the luxury of visiting the Middle Fork country and the central Idaho mountains do so at the expense of the native people who once lived in this region and who were forced to leave. Although Boyer supports designated wilderness, including the Frank Church ("They should have set aside more," he says), his perspective sours on the subject of commercial outfitting and the increasing number of outdoor enthusiasts who visit the Middle Fork. It's hard to blame him. While thousands of tourists with no vested interest in the land frolic down the river, eating prime rib and shooting each other with water guns, Boyer remembers that his own parents grew up knowing only what they learned in stories about the country their ancestors had inhabited for hundreds of generations.

Boyer still visits the places where his descendents once lived. "I go back to take my grandchildren, to make contact with my ancestors," he says, "to talk to the water, the plants, and the rocks." When asked about how the land has changed, Boyer can only wonder. After all, he never knew the land, at least not in the way his grandparents and their grandparents did. Isolated pockets of backcountry probably remain unchanged since the days of the Tukuduka. Other places, like those along the heavily used Middle Fork corridor, are trammeled and beaten down. The biggest change, of course, is that the people who lived there were long ago run out and fenced in.

The day I met Lionel Boyer, he wore dark glasses and a baseball cap. I never saw his eyes. We talked about how his family was uprooted from its homeland, how a way of life that had evolved over thousands of years had been stomped on. I asked him if there was any common ground between the experience of visitors to the Middle Fork country and the experience of the native people who once lived there. He paused and gave me a quizzical look. More silence passed between us, but in his facial expression I read an answer. Any non-native experience with the land of the Salmon River Mountains is based on the fact that Boyer's people are no longer there. There is no common ground. I regretted the arrogance of my question and, although I couldn't see his eyes, I imagined a tear.

Following Spread:
Low water in Lower Cliffside Rapid exposes metamorphic boulders and a jagged cliff wall etched with high water marks.

River Canyon

When working commercial trips there is precious little time for long hikes that afford a unique birds-eye view of the river. One afternoon in July of 2000, I led a group of clients to The Grotto at the base of Veil Falls, deep in Impassable Canyon. While the group returned to the boats, I scrambled across a series of ledges to a spectacular vista point. Looking downstream, the red splash of tiny boats exaggerates the vastness and depth of the canyon.

M.L.

Opposite:
Guide and passengers stare mesmerized at the sinuous walls of metamorphic rock that flank the river above Ship Island.

THREE WAYS OF A RIVER

David Wagoner

Sometimes, without a murmur, the river chooses
      the clearest channels, the easy ways
Downstream, dividing at islands equally, smoothly,
And meeting itself once more on the far side
      In a gather of seamless eddies
That blend so well, no ripples to break

Into light like fingerling taking their first mayflies
Or, again, it will rush at overhangs
And blunder constantly against bare stone,
Against some huge implacable rock-face
      To steepen and plunge, spring wide, go white,
And be dashed in tatters of spray, revolved and scattered

Like rain clouds pouring forward against a cliff
      In an endless storm of its own making,
While calmly a foot away lies the shape all water
Becomes if it flows aside into a pool,
      As still as the rock that holds it, as level
As if held cold to drink in these two hands.

Opposite:
Morning light reflects in a pool just above Redside
Rapid.

Following Spread:
Looking down on an outfitter group camped at Otter
Bar at the height of the summer season.

Perspectives

"I had been meaning to do that river for thirty years before I finally got it done—and it was one of those trips of a lifetime."

Jim Cannon
Salmon, ID

"Just majestic! You are part of it— not a spectator, but a participant. That alone is awesome."

Bob Bryant
Santa Barbara, CA

"The Middle Fork water is crystal clear; it is warm, there are no bugs, and the fishing is the best! There's nothing like a river trip. It's the only vacation trip I have done more than once."

Gary Rogers
Greenwich, CT

"I would rather go down the Middle Fork than go to Paris. It's a passion in my life. I know the day will come when I will not be able to do this trip any longer, but I hope that day is a long way off. I plan on doing it every year until I can't get on the boat anymore."

Bill Wexelblatt
Piedmont, CA

"All of our boating friends are busy professional people, and we go to the river because it is so different from our everyday lives. It's almost like a drug to us. All the scenery, beautiful nights, hot springs—we just don't have that around here. I don't know of anyplace else like it."

Ron Perry
Oklahoma City, OK

"In Kansas, we don't really have any wilderness recreation opportunities. On the Middle Fork the outfitters provide me with a chance to enjoy some of Idaho and that wilderness experience. It's great to get that first cup of coffee in the morning, look up at the ridge top, and marvel at the beauty of it all."

Charlie Brown
Wichita, KA

"The trip provided a perfect setting for rediscovery of laughter and playfulness that our usual lifestyles don't afford. I, for one, had greatly underestimated the rejuvenating power of the natural setting and social interaction this trip provided."

Hilary Fraser
Ithaca, NY

"It's been like a dream. Unfortunately, we all have to wake up."

Rick Donnalley
Marietta, GA

" I feel like I could use every adjective in the book to describe the trip. There was nothing about it we didn't love … everything from the scenery to the rafting and whitewater to the surprises around every corner. It was truly one of the best trips we have been on. We've been all around the world and this was different than any other trip we have ever taken."

Lara Courturier
Bristol, RI

"I miss the stars … It was the most relaxed I have ever been, and when you can say that while also whitewater rafting then you know it was a good trip."

Jerrod Courturier
Bristol, RI

"Take mountains, add whitewater, sprinkle in rocky mountain sheep, and rocks, then bake in the hot sun for six days with seven great guides. Yield—one fabulous trip."

Kerry Wilson
Pound Ridge, NY

"I miss the peacefulness, the quiet, the water. I live in a big city with 90,000 people. There is constant noise, but I have always said that I will never live anywhere until I can live on a river. My first trip was in 1975 and I just miss the river. It's a whole different world when you are on the river."

Maryvee Westland
Everett, WA

"The best thing is to float with knowledgeable guides. A river trip should be a bit of a learning experience and I learn something every time I go. And although I've floated just about all of the rivers that Bob [Sevy] runs, I like going back to the Middle Fork because I never get tired of it. It's not a river where you can say, 'Okay, I've done the Middle Fork.' Not for me, I always want to go back. I never get tired of it."

Pat Millington
Picabo, ID

"Weeks after the sudden passing of my father, I spent five days on the Middle Fork with a group of my oldest and dearest friends. Noting the peaceful grin on my face as we drifted through a flat section near the Flying B Ranch, my friend Brayton turned to me and said in the most endearing tone, 'Your father would be so proud of you for doing this.' I knew he was right. Dad lived for this stuff and the experience recalled a flood of outdoor memories that we shared together. Memories interspersed with moments of exhilaration, adventure, and relaxation. My days on the Middle Fork reminded me that it is okay to experience laughter and happiness during what had been the saddest days of my entire life. When I look back on this difficult time, I'm glad that I will be able to include the radiant memory of the breathtaking river country of the Middle Fork."

Margot Higgins
Bozeman, MT

Many tributaries tumble into Impassable
Canyon. The grotto at the base of Mist Falls,
however, is my favorite. One

Mist Falls
afternoon, I hiked to the waterfall to
create this image showing the sweep of the
canyon and the curtain of water lit by the
slanting afternoon light.

M.L.

Waterfall On a climbing trip with my family, I discovered this waterfall hidden far up a tributary drainage to Impassable Canyon. In October of 2000, I returned to the location for this image which, to me, represents the hidden gems found only through extended exploration into the deepest reaches of the Frank Church River of No Return Wilderness.

M.L.

Top to Bottom:
Sunset reflects against rain falling from a passing thundercloud.

A waxing moon rises over a ridgeline of ponderosa pine.

A family of bighorn sheep picks its way along the cliffs across from Grassy Flat Camp.

Opposite:
The jagged skyline downstream from Wilson Creek etches its silhouette against the stars.

Hailed as either Redside, Weber, or Corkscrew, this Class IV rapid in Impassable Canyon offers a challenge to any boater.

Running the Flood

by Peter Gibbs

The Middle Fork drainage had an unusually heavy snowpack in 1982, and in late June, a full week of rain caused it to melt rapidly. The gauge at Middle Fork Lodge reported the river at seven feet and rising. The Middle Fork, a small, rocky river running through a narrow canyon, was going to be changed drastically by the coming flood.

During a break in the weather, John Cole, Steve Hamel, and I flew into Indian Creek Guard Station. Knowing that the river would be frighteningly fast and unforgiving, we elected to bypass the steep, rocky section from Boundary Creek to Indian Creek.

Having worked the Middle Fork of the Salmon for many of the 18 years I'd been guiding river trips, I could claim a lot of high-water experience there, as well as in Cataract and Grand Canyons on the Colorado, and on the Columbia in Canada. John and Steve were experienced boatmen, as well.

We rigged our 16-foot inflatable oar-powered rafts and signed up for camps with Eli, the ranger. Our choices were based on height above the river, since many of the camps would be under water. Our twelve passengers flew in about noon, resplendent in their new camping togs. They milled around grumbling, unhappy about missing the first 25 miles of river. The canyon is wide at Indian Creek, the river calm and deceptively pacific. They didn't see the danger.

We set off in a drizzle. The water was pushy, but the rocks were all covered. Instead of dodging boulders, we fought big eddy lines and powerful, confused currents. At Ski-Jump rapid, the canyon narrowed markedly. The river ran down a long chute and crashed into the left wall. A monstrous reflex wave extended out into midstream. With the rapid roaring in my ears, I pulled hard right, just missing a certain boat flip in the wave. As my boat shot between the wave and a rock pinnacle, it wallowed suddenly, tipping dangerously in the violent, bubble-filled water. Then we were through, shaking and laughing—but I had realized that every stroke of the oars would be crucial. Decisions had to be made quickly and actions taken without hesitation.

At Middle Fork Lodge we skirted the left bank, just passing under the footbridge. Water was brushing the center of the span. A few more feet and the bridge would be in danger.

At Hood Ranch, a large flat with a hot spring, we tied all of the boats together well above the river. Steve pushed a stick into the ground at water level to measure changes.

During dinner there was some grousing because the river didn't look dangerous to the customers. Then, just before dark, debris began going by. River bags, food boxes, and oars floated around the corner and out of sight. Someone upstream had suffered a bad wreck. The seriousness of what we were undertaking began to sink in. We heard no more complaints.

Opposite:
A cautious kayaker wisely avoids the big holes of Wall Creek Rapid.

In the morning Steve checked his stick; the water had risen another foot. We tied our loads down carefully, preparing for a tip-over. It was raining again, so everyone geared up with rain suits under lifejackets. We instructed our passengers in the art of bailing (these were the days before self-bailing rubber boats were available).

It was cold, nervous running. The river looked foreign, the shore going by in a blur. Only the largest boulders protruded above water. The few eddies were powerful, with dangerous shear-lines. The river crashed into the corners, eroding the banks, pulling whole trees into the current. Our boats wallowed and spun. The customers bailed almost continuously, trying to help us maintain control of the heavy rafts.

The rapids we usually watched for were washed out. The spots that threatened us were new and unexpected, and the river was getting stronger and wilder with every increase in water volume. We ran on adrenaline—going from corner to corner at high speed; looking ahead, setting up, and looking ahead again. Great boils rose suddenly under the boats, throwing them to one side or the other. A mistake would be disastrous. The river was mostly recent snowmelt, and if a boat tipped over, we would float miles in ice-cold water before getting to shore. Hypothermia was a serious danger.

Camp that night was at Rock Island, on an inside corner just below another rapid. It would take a gut-wrenching pull-in for us to land the rafts. To ensure our making it, we decided to off-load the passengers above the rapid. We pulled out of the current into a normally placid eddy to find it chaotic: Waves rose and crashed unpredictably all around us, bouncing the boats wildly against a rock ledge. Getting everyone off the boats and onto the ledge was frightening. Anyone falling in would likely have been crushed between the boats and the ledge.

John and I bounced helplessly around the eddy while Steve took the customers down to camp and set up to catch the boats. If we missed the landing, Steve and the customers would be stranded; we wouldn't be able to get back to them. One at a time we ran the boats down, threw our bowlines to Steve, and muscled the boats ashore.

A good shot of whiskey helped to calm us down as we unloaded the boats and discussed the danger. We had to keep our passengers safe, and had to convey how close to the edge we were running without panicking them. We were beginning to feel the effects of the trip. Our nerves were frayed and our arms and backs were stiff from pulling full strength on the oars all day. We didn't know what obstacles lay ahead.

It rained again that night and by morning the river had risen another foot. The boats, at the end of their tethers, banged roughly against one another in heavy current. The customers boarded reluctantly. Their new clothes were muddy and wet. They were cold, dejected, and frightened. We were frightened, too. The river was getting rougher and more unpredictable with each passing mile, each side stream that entered, each ton of added snowmelt.

We pulled in next to a 22-foot sweep boat at Tappan Ranch, and Randy Stone came out to greet us. Randy, a big strapping man with years of Middle Fork experience, told us this was supposed to be his third night's camp, but it was the first place he had been able to stop since he put on the river. The sweep was the gear boat for his party. He didn't know where they were. He had decided he would fly out the next day from the Flying B Ranch, eleven miles downstream.

John, Steve, and I talked it over. We couldn't afford a tip-over. It was just too dangerous; we had too much responsibility for our passengers. We would fly them out at the Flying B as well.

Our disheveled customers gathered around us, shivering in the rain. I told them of our decision, explaining that below the Flying B, the canyon was much narrower and the rapids more serious. No one objected. Hearing Randy's story and seeing how worried he was had spooked everyone. I was thoroughly relieved. I didn't know what the boss would say, but I didn't want to be responsible for losing someone's life.

When we pulled in the next morning at the Flying B, several other parties were rolling up boats and loading equipment into Cessnas for the flight out. Steve called on the Flying B's radiophone to let the boss know what we were doing.

"Well," John asked, "what now? Do we send the boats out on the plane or run them out empty?"

I thought about it. We had thirty miles to go to the confluence with the Main Salmon, and it would go very fast. We only had ourselves to look out for; it would be a fantastic adventure and we would probably never have another chance to run the Middle Fork at such high water. Bernard Creek, just below us,

had the last airstrip on the river. We would be hanging it out a long way. I gulped and said, "We're here. We might as well see it." My stomach tightened up when they didn't object.

We sent out most of the equipment, wanting boats light enough to maneuver and heavy enough not to flip in a breaking wave. We tied our loads down as we watched the planes taking off, carrying our passengers to the safety of the worka-day world. Nervously, we set off for the adventure of a lifetime.

There is a feeling to a river in flood, a river that is rising, confined to a canyon too narrow to contain it. It buffets the boats. It is inconsistent, chaotic. Waves appear suddenly out of nowhere. They rise and crash, throwing the boats from side to side, twisting them out of line with the waves. It took all our strength to keep the boats out of trouble, and to keep them close enough together to monitor what happened to each other yet far enough apart to see ahead and maneuver.

We stopped to look at Haystack, a complex rapid littered with boulders. Massive holes punctuated the river, huge waves rebounded from a line of boul-ders; but there was a narrow current, like a raised road running through, if we could stay on it. Tentativeness would spell disaster. Each stroke had to be quick

and full strength. The boats rose and fell in overpowering swell, inches from terrible holes and enormous boulders. Past the worst, we bailed frantically, preparing for whatever came next.

Farther on, below Jack Creek Rapid, a dejected group of boaters was huddled around a fire drying off and warming up. They had flipped two boats in Haystack and chased them four miles downstream through several more rapids. It made us think. It made us watch each other more closely.

At Survey Creek the canyon takes two sharp turns that the flooding river refused to follow. A heavy reflex wave piled off a cliff, cutting off the right side of the river. On the left a heavily forested point was under water. The river ran pell-mell through it, raising spray where logs and other debris were jammed against trees. Getting strained through there would be certain death. I rowed frantically, skirting the trees, taking the edge of the wave. Then I bailed and looked back for John and Steve.

Big Creek was flooding, adding to the river's size. It marked the beginning of Impassable Canyon and the end of the foot trail along the river. Up to this point, if we found ourselves in over our heads, we could have pulled the boats far up on shore, tied them off, and hiked back to the Flying B. Now we were totally committed; the only way out was the river.

Granite walls rose ominously around us. The biggest rapids in the canyon were ahead. We pulled in above the worst of them and scrambled down the bank to look.

Sevy's Rock was a network of behemoth boulders and holes big enough to swallow our boats whole. There was a narrow channel on the right, if we could get to it. I entered center and rowed hard to the right, lining up for a narrow slot that dropped over a line of boulders, a slot I could not afford to miss. Anyone thrown

Flood water drowns shoreline shrubs at Funston Camp during a high spring runoff.

Opposite:
Spring rafters take a ride in Rubber Rapid.

out of the boat here would float through Red Side and Weber, two more very big rapids. The slot was nearly invisible from above, just a small bulge of laminar flow in the torrent. I made my decision and pushed toward the bulge, trying to gain momentum and forcing the boat to the slot. Wild spray covered me as I dropped into the maelstrom. A monstrous hole gaped on my left. Granite boulders threatened my right. The force of the current flushed me through. When I could, I jumped into the bilge and bailed wildly, already thinking ahead to Rubber, probably the biggest rapid in the canyon.

Above Rubber, a quick turn cuts off any chance to see ahead. The canyon narrows dramatically here, and fallen boulders have dammed up the river. A string of huge standing waves was running down the center, the fourth wave breaking back violently on itself at unpredictable intervals. There were only a few seconds to size it up before we were in it. Steve and I pulled with all our might into

Kayakers negotiate Cliffside Rapid (above) and the churning whitewater of Rubber Rapid (below).

Closing Spread:
The last rays of sun illuminate wisps of rain falling like fire from a passing thundercloud above Wilson Creek.

pounding, confused water on the far right. John got sucked into the middle. Out of control, his boat burst over the waves. The fourth wave broke as he hit it. We could see the entire bottom of his boat for a second. I turned my boat, preparing to chase after him. Then his boat slapped down, still upright—a very lucky result.

Below us lay the section I most feared, where sharp, black cliffs of gneiss and schist start at the edge of a river that is extremely narrow, dangerously fast, and pocked with house-size boulders. The canyon twists and turns, cutting off our view and creating giant waves and over-powering currents. We would have very little time to react to what was coming.

At an extremely constricted place above Hancock Rapid, a sharp turn kept me from seeing ahead and I was taken completely by surprise. At a normally calm place, a massive wave pounded off the left wall, extending most of the way across the river. There was no time to be frightened, only time to react. I strained with all my might, just missing a sure tip-over, and shot into a jumble of waves and holes— the rapid itself. I was buffeted and smashed violently. Out of control, I dropped into holes and crashed through waves, my boat filling with water. There was no way to move out of trouble. It took all my strength to keep the boat pointed straight into whatever came. The weight of the water in my boat was probably what kept it upright.

Devil's Tooth, House of Rocks, and Jump Off rapids were ahead, but I couldn't find them. All my landmarks were under water; I didn't recognize any of the drops. Things were happening very fast. Reacting frantically, I dodged a massive pour-over. The hole below it churned and roared within feet of my boat.

I was disoriented, and I could taste the fear. I knew it wasn't far to the confluence with the Main Salmon, but didn't know whether we would come to something unrunnable, a place where a constriction wave extended completely across the river. Nowhere was there slow water, a place to pull over and look.

I continued to work from corner to corner, looking ahead, setting up, and rowing with ever-decreasing strength. I rowed left around a violent corner that I recognized: Goat Creek. And ahead, just in sight, loomed the Main Salmon.

The confluence looked strange. The Main Salmon was also in flood, pushing a terrific volume of water upstream into the Middle Fork, forcing it back and creating an eddy-fence big enough to flip a boat. We had to make the landing just below the confluence on the opposite side of the Main Salmon, but there was a long chain of huge waves leading past the landing. I reacted feverishly, knowing I had to survive the eddy-fence and the violent force of a river running over 90,000 feet per second. If I flipped here, the boat would be lost and I would have to swim for shore in turbulent, unforgiving water. I pulled to the upstream side of the confluence and started across, rowing crosswise to the waves, knowing I could afford neither to tip nor to miss the landing.

Near the end of my strength, I made it to shore, leapt off the boat, grabbed the bowline, and pulled the boat in. Panting, exhausted, I watched as John and Steve made the crossing, ready to make chase if necessary. Fortunately, it wasn't necessary.

We popped a beer in celebration and slapped each other on the back. We'd done it. We'd had a harrowing adventure, but we'd made it. We'd run the Middle Fork at a higher water level than we were likely ever to see again. Our driver told us the river was now over ten feet on the gauge. It had taken about three hours of intense concentration and effort to run 30 miles in extreme conditions. It was an adventure that none of us will ever forget.

Contributors

Cort Conley   A licensed boatman since 1968, Cort Conley lives in Idaho, where he writes about river history and directs the literature program for the Idaho Commission on the Arts.

Peter Gibbs   Peter Gibbs' first river boating experience was in 1958, when his junior high class ran Glen Canyon. He started working on rivers in college and has guided in Idaho, Utah, and Colorado, including five years as a guide for Grand Canyon Expeditions. Since 1966, he has worked for Sevy Guide Service and Hughes River Expeditions in Idaho. In 1965, he created the "Gibbs Ascender," a mechanical prussic device used around the world by spelunkers, mountain climbers, and rescue personnel. Peter holds a Bachelor's degree in physics and a Doctorate in mechanical engineering from the University of Utah.

Jim Harper   Jim Harper, a native of Idaho, was born in 1965 in Sun Valley—a place that kindled his love of the outdoors. He has been a river guide on the Middle Fork of the Salmon since he was seventeen. He holds a bachelor's degree in art from Western State College and a Masters from Boise State University. He teaches art at Riverstone Community School in Boise, where he lives with his wife Jill and their a 20-month old son, Harrison.

Greg Moore   A former river guide, Greg Moore works as a newspaper reporter in Ketchum, Idaho. He has kayaked throughout the Western states, Alaska, and South America. He has guided commercial raft trips on the Main and Middle Forks of the Salmon, and kayak trips on the rivers of Chile. Greg grew up in Connecticut, knowing all along that he belonged in the West.

Erik Leidecker   Erik Leidecker is a year-round mountain guide and freelance writer who lives with his wife Gretchen and baby daughter Sascha in Hailey, Idaho. His first experiences on the Middle Fork included a two-day backpacking trip when he was nine and a flip in Rubber when he was ten. Since then, he has occasionally worked as a guide on the Middle Fork and manages to squeeze in at least one trip every summer—some of them with his brother Matt.

William Studebaker   William Studebaker is a poet and writer who occasionally teaches literature and creative writing at Idaho State University. He is a columnist for *The Times-News* (Outdoor Page). William was born in Salmon, Idaho, and has "always" been a whitewater and wilderness enthusiast. His books, which typically have outdoor, landscape, or socio-ecological themes, include *Passions We Desire*, *Short of a Good Promise*, *Travelers in an Antique Land*, and *River Religion*. He is currently at work on a manuscript about a kayaking journey with his son in Northern Greenland, and a collection of poems about small western towns. He lives near Twin Falls, Idaho, with his wife, Judy.

Clarence Stilwill   After running the Middle Fork with a private party in 1972, Clarence Stilwill came back, quit his job and was working as a licensed guide by 1973. He spent the next ten years guiding on all the major rivers of the Northwest until circumstances forced him to rejoin the "grown-up" world. First creating a building company then a publishing company. Today, in partnership with his wife Tona he raises specialty organic vegetables on an ancient homestead site near Fairfield, Idaho. Clarence says that of all the rivers that he has run, the Middle Fork still courses through him as deeply as it does the wild canyons of the Frank Church Wilderness, and someday it will carry him home to the Western Sea. "Or at least to an irrigation ditch somewhere in Washington State."

David Wagoner   David Wagoner has published seventeen books of poetry and ten novels, one of which—*The Escape Artist*—was made into a movie by Francis Ford Coppola. He has been nominated twice for the National Book Award, won the Lilly Prize (1991), and the William Stafford Memorial Award. He was a chancellor of the Academy of American Poets for 23 years. David has taught at the University of Washington since 1954.

A special thanks to the following outfitters for their support.

Action Whitewater Adventures
P.O. Box 1634
Provo, UT 84603
800.453.1482
www.riverguide.com

Adventure! Sun Valley River Co.
2115 S.W. Ave.
Portland, OR 97225
503.292.9170
www.sunvalleyriver.com

Aggipah River Tours
P.O. Box 425
Salmon, ID 83467
208.756.4167
bill@aggipah.com

ARTA
24000 Casa Loma Road
Groveland, CA 95321
800.323.2782
www.arta.org

Canyons Incorporated
P.O. Box 823
McCall, ID 83638
888.634.2600
www.CanyonsInc.com

Custom River Tours
P.O. Box 7071
Boise, ID 83707
800.432.4611
www.selway.net

Echo: The Wilderness Company
6529 Telegraph Ave.
Oakland, CA 94609
800.652.3246
www.echotrips.com

Far and Away Adventures
P.O. Box 54
Sun Valley, ID 83353
800.232.8588
www.far-away.com

Helfrich River Outfitters Inc.
37855 Shenandoah Loop
Springfield, OR 97478
800.507.9889
www.helfrichoutfitter.com

Hughes River Expeditions, Inc.
P.O. Box 217
Cambridge, ID 83610
800.262.1882
www.hughesriver.com

Idaho River Journeys
P.O. Box 1415
Salmon, ID 83476
888.997.8399
www.IdahoRiverJourneys.com

Mackay Wilderness River Trips
4115 Wright St.
Boise, ID 83705
800.635.5336
www.mackayriver.com

Middle Fork Rapid Transit
2402 N. 26th St.
Boise, ID 83702
888.433.5628
www.idahoraftadventure.com

Middle Fork River Expeditions
P.O. Box 199
Stanley, ID 83278
800.801.5146
www.idahorivers.com

Middle Fork River Tours
P.O. Box 2222
Hailey, ID 83333
800.445.9738
www.middlefork.com

Middle Fork Wilderness Outfitters
P.O. Box 575
Ketchum, ID 83340
208.726.5999
800.726.0575
www.idahorapids.com

Oars*Dories
P.O. Box 216
Atlantaville, CA 95221
800.877.3679
www.oars.com

Rocky Mountain River Tours
P.O. Box 8596
Boise, ID 83707
208.345.2400
www.rafttrips.com

ROW (River Odysseys West)
P.O. Box 579
Coeur d'Alene, ID 83816
800.451.6034
www.rowinc.com

Sevy Guide Service
P.O. Box 24
Stanley, ID 83278
208.774.2200
www.sevyguide.com

Schaefers Guide Service
P.O. Box 34
Vida, OR 97488
541.896.3789
sgsfish@aol.com

Solitude River Trips
P.O. Box 907
Merlin, OR 97532
800.396.1776
www.rivertrips.com

Warren River Expeditions
P.O. Box 1375
Salmon, ID 83467
800.765.0421
www.raftidaho.com

Wilderness River Outfitters
P.O. Box 72
Lemhi, ID 83465
800.252.6581
www.wildernessriver.com

Index of Photographs

All of the above photographs by Matt Leidecker are available for purchase, including special limited edition prints of select images. For information and rates, contact Matt Leidecker Photography at 208.720.4712 or visit www.middleforkbook.com.

Acknowledgements

First and foremost I want to thank my family for their understanding and support and, maybe even more important, for living an alternative lifestyle. In addition, I want to thank all of my climbing, hiking, skiing, boating, and general adventuring partners for putting up with the demands of having a trigger-happy photographer along for the ride.

A special thanks to fellow river guides of the past five years for tolerating my absence in the kitchen, and for pointing out shots I just shouldn't miss. Thank you to the writers and artists—Clarence, Cort, David, Bill, Greg, Erik, Pete, and Jim—for adding elements to the book that cannot be expressed in photos. For the financial support of Karl, Doug, Dennis, Fred, and Joel, I am immensely grateful. The design, editorial, and production team at Sun Valley Press has done an exceptional job with the book. In addition, I would like to thank the guide, client, and private boater interviewees, Dharma Designs, F-Stop, Kate O, Tony F, Pro Photo, Middle Fork Outfitters, Sheri and the F.S. gals, Schaefers crew, Canyons crew, and the Midd Boyz.